Ancient Echoes: Embracing Egyptian Wisdom in Our Modern World

Myrddin Sage

Published by Myrddin Sage, 2024.

While every precaution has been taken in the preparation of this book, the publisher assumes no responsibility for errors or omissions, or for damages resulting from the use of the information contained herein.

ANCIENT ECHOES: EMBRACING EGYPTIAN WISDOM IN OUR MODERN WORLD

First edition. August 26, 2024.

ISBN: 979-8227730015

Written by Myrddin Sage.

Table of Contents

Ancient Echoes: Embracing Egyptian Wisdom in Our Modern World

Discover How Time-Honored Mythologies Can Transform Your Everyday Reality

Preface

"The only thing new in the world is the history you do not know." – Harry Truman.

In our fast-paced modern lives, where technology and current events often dominate our attention, the whispers of ancient wisdom from the pages of our forgotten books and the echoes of our cultural heritage can still be heard. This book is an invitation to rediscover and apply the profound insights of Egyptian mythology, making them not just a relic of the past, but a relevant and practical guide for our contemporary existence.

At the heart of this exploration is a bridge between past and present, where timeless tales from ancient Egypt are not just stories but lessons that resonate with the challenges and questions we face today. From personal growth to professional development, the mythologies of pharaohs, gods, and goddesses offer more than historical intrigue—they provide frameworks for understanding human nature and guiding our decisions.

The inspiration for this book came from a series of lectures I attended and my travels through Egypt. Standing before the awe-inspiring pyramids of Giza, I felt a profound connection to a past that seemed both distant and yet strangely familiar. Conversations with fellow travelers, many of whom were fascinated by these ancient stories but struggled to see their relevance today, convinced me that there was a bridge to be built.

Many of you might find yourselves in similar situations. Perhaps you're seeking deeper meaning in your career or at a crossroads in your personal life. Like a young professional I met during my travels, who felt disconnected from her cultural roots but yearned for a sense of purpose that transcended her everyday tasks. Or a retired teacher who found solace and inspiration in mythology during a particularly challenging time in his life. These stories propelled me to delve deeper and bring these ancient narratives into conversations around modern-day dilemmas.

My journey was enriched by numerous scholars and enthusiasts of Egyptian culture whose insights appear throughout this book. Their perspectives have been instrumental in shaping the content and ensuring its accuracy and depth.

I want to express my sincere gratitude to you for choosing to spend your time with these pages. Your curiosity about life's deeper questions breathes new life into these ancient stories. This book is crafted for those who love to learn, who find joy in the exchange of ideas across time, and who seek to infuse their daily lives with the wisdom that has guided humanity for millennia.

This book does not require prior knowledge of Egyptian mythology; instead, it invites you on a journey from curiosity to deep understanding. By its conclusion, you should be able to see the historical significance and the personal relevance of these ancient myths.

Thank you for your purchase and for embarking on this journey with me. I invite you now to turn the page and begin exploring how Egyptian wisdom can transform your everyday reality into something truly extraordinary.

Chapter 1: Echoes from the Desert: Why Egyptian Mythology Matters Today

In the heart of Cairo, where the cacophony of car horns and street vendors blends into a symphony of modern chaos, Sarah found herself walking the narrow lanes that still whispered tales of ancient times. The sun hung low in the sky, casting long shadows that danced around her feet as if pointing her toward an old bookstore tucked away behind a string of spice shops. The scent of cumin and cardamom filled the air, mingling with the dust stirred up by passing feet.

Inside, the bookstore was a sanctuary of silence, starkly contrasting the roar outside its walls. Sarah ran her fingers over spines of books as aged as the myths they spoke about. She pulled out a tome on Egyptian mythology, its cover worn and pages yellowed with time.

As she flipped through it, her mind wandered to the challenges weighing on her — an overwhelming job, a fracturing relationship, and a pervasive sense of being lost in an ever-accelerating world.

The chapter on Ma'at caught her eye — the ancient Egyptian concept of truth, balance, harmony, and order. It was said that Ma'at was not just a goddess but also a principle that maintained the universe. The Egyptians believed that for their society to thrive rather than survive amid chaos and disorder, Ma'at had to be upheld in every aspect of daily life.

Sarah sat by a window in an old wooden chair, looking out onto the bustling street. She thought about how disconnected modern life seemed from those ancient principles—how everything moved so fast there was hardly a moment to seek balance or reflect on one's actions. Her phone buzzed relentlessly in her bag, with emails demanding immediate answers and messages dotted with urgent exclamation marks.

A cat sauntered in through an open door at the back of the shop and jumped onto her lap uninvited but welcome. Its purring offered comfort as she pondered how little time she spent on things that brought harmony into her life compared to those that fostered discord.

Outside again, Sarah let her thoughts drift back to Ma'at as she navigated through crowds moving like torrents around rocks in rapid waters. How could one find balance when surrounded by such relentless noise and demand? Was it even possible anymore?

As dusk settled over Cairo's skyline, turning it from orange to pink and then deep blue before succumbing to night's blackness, adorned only by scattered lights like distant stars, Sarah wondered whether looking back at these ancient ways could indeed help navigate through today's turbulences.

Could understanding these age-old concepts provide guidance amidst our contemporary existential crises?

Unveiling Timeless Wisdom in a Fast-Paced World

Rapid advancements in technology and constant shifts in our societal structures often leave us grappling with a profound sense of disorientation and emptiness. Amidst this chaos, the ancient wisdom of Egyptian mythology emerges not as mere stories from the past but as vital insights that are remarkably relevant today.

This chapter delves into how these age-old narratives can guide us through modern existential challenges, illuminating paths toward balance and harmony.

With its rich tapestry of gods, goddesses, and mythical narratives, Egyptian mythology offers more than just historical interest; it provides a framework to understand the timeless cycles of life, death, and rebirth. These themes are central to ancient spiritual practices and incredibly pertinent to our contemporary quest for meaning. The stories from the deserts of Egypt teach us the importance of maintaining cosmic order and the inevitability of transformation. These concepts can help us cope with today's world's inevitable changes and disruptions.

Bridging Ancient Sands to Modern Chaos

The silent expanses of the Egyptian deserts starkly contrast our noisy, bustling city lives. Yet, both landscapes share underlying themes of survival, adaptation, and renewal. This chapter will explore how embracing these themes can offer deeper insights into living harmoniously amidst chaos. Understanding how ancient Egyptians perceived life and the afterlife, we can gain perspectives that foster resilience against modern stresses.

Our journey through Egyptian mythology will reveal how these ancient beliefs reflect on life's cyclical nature. Recognizing this can change how we perceive our personal challenges and societal upheavals — not as isolated incidents but as part of a larger, enduring rhythm. The myths teach us about **balance** — Ma'at in Egyptian culture — which was essential for sustaining the universe's order. Today, this principle can inspire us to find equilibrium in our fast-paced lives filled with digital distractions and relentless change.

Life Lessons from Legends

As we delve into stories such as those of Isis, Osiris, and Horus, we uncover layers of symbolism applicable to our lives. For instance, Osiris's death and resurrection echo the transformative power of facing life's darker moments—an encouraging metaphor for personal growth through adversity. This chapter will highlight such stories to show that renewal follows loss and that continuity can be found even in disruption.

Moreover, understanding these myths helps cultivate a mindset that values **harmony over** chaos. It guides us in personal interactions and broader societal engagements and empowers us to navigate life's complexities with grace and wisdom.

Embracing Cosmic Order Amidst Technological Surge

Today's technological surge might seem like a world apart from the slow changes of ancient times. However, the Egyptian emphasis on cosmic order provides a valuable lens through which to view our relationship with technology. It invites us to seek harmony within ourselves and in how we interact with our environment and technological tools.

By integrating lessons from Egyptian mythology into our daily lives, we learn to approach life's uncertainties not with fear but with a poised readiness for transformation. This approach does not merely help us cope. Still, it enables us to thrive by turning challenges into opportunities for growth and self-discovery.

This chapter sets the stage for a transformative journey through "Echoes of the Ancients," where each page promises knowledge and practical wisdom applicable to various aspects of modern living. By revisiting these ancient stories, we do not escape from reality; instead, we better equip ourselves to deal with it—drawing strength from myths that have survived the sands of time.

Understanding Modern Existential Challenges Through Egyptian Mythology

Today's world buzzes with technology and constant communication, starkly contrasting the expansive silence of the ancient Egyptian deserts. This juxtaposition reveals a deeper connection between our modern lives and ancient practices. The Egyptians found profound spirituality in the isolation of their desert landscapes, which helped them develop a rich mythology that still resonates with themes applicable in our times.

In the hustle of urban life, one can feel lost, akin to a small boat adrift in a vast ocean without a compass. Egyptian mythology, rooted in the clarity and vastness of the desert, teaches us the importance of finding our inner compass, our personal guiding North Star. This mythology offers stories and tools for finding direction in the noise surrounding us.

For instance, consider the Egyptian concept of Ma'at, which represents truth, balance, and order. In a world where misinformation can spread quickly, understanding and embracing Ma'at's principles can help us discern truth and maintain ethical standards. The Egyptians saw Ma'at as essential to the harmony of the universe. This concept can help us navigate daily chaos toward a more balanced life.

Similarly, the silence of the desert, often reflected in the calm demeanor of the gods and goddesses in Egyptian myths, invites us to find quiet in our lives amidst the urban clamor. Just as the desert's vastness offered the Egyptians a physical and metaphorical space to reflect and rejuvenate, we, too, can seek moments of silence to gain clarity.

Egyptian mythology, with its deep roots in the serene desert landscapes, provides timeless wisdom that helps us navigate the existential challenges of our noisy, modern world.

The Cycle of Life, Death, and Rebirth in Our Understanding

Egyptian mythology is rife with themes of life, death, and rebirth. These themes are not merely historical curiosities but hold profound insights into the nature of existence. The stories of gods like Osiris, who dies and is reborn, mirror the cycles we see in our lives—from the natural world's seasons to our personal experiences of loss and renewal.

Why do these ancient narratives about cycles resonate so profoundly with us? They remind us that endings are also beginnings—just as the Nile's flooding was seen as both a destructive and a nurturing force. This cyclical understanding can help us cope with personal and collective crises, offering a perspective that every end leads to a new beginning.

In exploring the concept of cosmic order, or Ma'at, we see how the ancients perceived a deeply interconnected universe, where every action contributed to the balance and order of the whole. This perspective can be transformative in our modern world, where individual actions seem small and insignificant.

Think of the Pharaoh as both a political and spiritual leader tasked with maintaining Ma'at. In our lives, we, too, have roles that contribute to societal balance, whether we are aware of them or not. Embracing this can empower us to live more purposefully.

Could understanding these ancient cycles and our role in cosmic balance lead us to more fulfilling lives?

Balancing Modern Life with Ancient Wisdom

In today's fast-paced world, filled with rapid technological advancements, the ancient Egyptian emphasis on balance and harmony is more relevant than ever. The myths of Egypt show us that balance is not static but a dynamic equilibrium that must be continually adjusted, much like balancing on a boat rocked by waves.

The story of the god Horus balancing his roles as a sky god and protector demonstrates the need for maintaining harmony between different aspects of life. This balance is crucial in our modern lives, where we juggle multiple responsibilities and roles.

Consider Ma'at again, not just as a principle but as a way of life. Integrating balance into our daily routine can help us manage and mitigate the stress of constant change and the barrage of information in the digital age.

Reflecting on these principles can offer a living framework that respects our advancements and our need for inner peace. We can cultivate a life that honors progress and stability by applying ancient wisdom to modern challenges.

By embracing the ancient Egyptian principles of balance and harmony, we can better navigate the complexities of modern life, ensuring that we maintain our equilibrium amidst constant change.

In the vast tapestry of modern existence, where technological marvels and societal changes often lead to a disconnection from our roots, the ancient wisdom of Egyptian mythology emerges as a guiding light. The stories and symbols from millennia ago are not mere relics of the past but vital tools that provide ***profound insights*** into the existential challenges we face today. From the chaos of noisy urban environments to the quest for meaning amid rapid change, these age-old themes resonate with striking relevance.

Understanding the cycles of life, death, and rebirth central to Egyptian lore helps us appreciate the natural rhythms of our own lives. Just as the sun god Ra dies each evening and is reborn at dawn, we too can find hope and renewal in our daily struggles and triumphs. This perspective encourages resilience and a deeper connection to the world around us, offering solace in times of personal upheaval.

Moreover, the Egyptian emphasis on *Ma'at*, or cosmic order and balance, is a crucial reminder of the need for harmony in our lives. In an age where imbalance manifests as stress, burnout, and ecological crisis, these ancient teachings urge us to seek equilibrium in our interactions with nature, technology, and each other. By embracing these principles, we enhance our well-being and contribute to a more balanced and sustainable world.

As we progress through this book, each chapter will build on these foundational ideas, exploring how other aspects of Egyptian mythology can illuminate various facets of modern life. You will discover how these timeless narratives can help cultivate leadership qualities, foster creativity, enhance relationships, and more.

The journey ahead promises a deeper understanding of a fascinating ancient civilization and practical wisdom that can transform your everyday reality. By integrating these age-old lessons into your life, you will be better equipped to navigate the complexities of the modern world with grace and wisdom.

Let us continue to explore together how the echoes of the ancients can resonate in our lives today, enriching our experience and guiding us toward a more enlightened existence.

Chapter 2: Revisiting the Ancients: Unveiling the True Relevance of Egyptian Myths

Sarah sat in the dusty warmth of a small Cairo café, nestled among the labyrinthine streets that sprawl like the roots of an ancient sycamore. Her eyes, reflecting a tumult of thoughts as vibrant as the city itself, scanned a tattered book on Egyptian mythology. The scent of strong coffee mingled with the aroma of baked clay from the sun-baked streets outside.

Sarah was an expatriate teacher. Her days were usually filled with the eager faces of students learning English, their curious and sprightly minds. But today was different. Today, she pondered over Osiris and Isis, deities wrapped in tales as old as time itself. She sought answers not just in myths but in life's fabric.

Her brother back home was battling a severe illness, his life hanging by a thread as fragile as those that once bound Osiris. The story of Isis gathering Osiris's scattered pieces to restore him resonated deeply with her. Wasn't she, too, trying to gather the scattered hopes and fortify her family?

A waiter clinked a cup on her table, breaking her reverie momentarily. She smiled faintly, thanking him before diving back into her thoughts. The streets buzzed with life outside; Cairo never paused, much like the swirling chaos she felt inside.

She thought about how myths reflect our deepest fears and highest hopes—universal emotions etched into stories from when gods walked among men. Could these ancient narratives offer solace or wisdom for her brother's ordeal? Or were they mere echoes of human fragility echoed through millennia?

As Sarah sipped her coffee, which was now cooling down to mere warmth matching the descending sun outside, she realized how intertwined our lives are with those of the ancients. Their stories were not just relics but reflections mirrored in modern upheavals—personal and societal.

She closed her book softly, contemplating whether understanding these myths could help reshape our perception during crises. Do we dismiss these stories as irrelevant because we fear confronting their underlying truths about our existence?

Are We Missing the Message Hidden in Ancient Myths?

When we think of Egyptian mythology, images of gods with animal heads and tales of the underworld often come to mind, dismissed by many as relics of a civilization long past. Yet, beneath these seemingly enigmatic stories lie profound insights into human nature and society that are as relevant today as they were thousands of years ago. This chapter seeks to bridge the gap between ancient wisdom and modern relevance, illustrating how Egyptian myths can illuminate our contemporary experiences and challenges.

Misconceptions abound about the relevance of Egyptian mythology. Many dismiss these stories as outdated or irrelevant, viewing them as complex narratives with little application to today's world. However, this perspective must include the depth and universality of the emotions and experiences depicted in these ancient tales. By unpacking these misconceptions, we begin to see the richness of Egyptian mythology and its potential to offer valuable lessons in our lives.

Unearthing Universal Emotions

Egyptian myths are steeped in themes of life, death, loyalty, betrayal, and love—universal experiences that resonate across time and culture. These stories are historical records and expressions of the human condition. As we explore these themes, we'll discover that the ancient Egyptians dealt with many of the same feelings and dilemmas we face today. Their struggles and triumphs offer us a mirror to reflect on our lives.

Reflecting on Modern Relevance

Egyptian mythology can provide a stable foundation for understanding our societal upheavals in a world that seems increasingly volatile and uncertain. The myths teach resilience and adaptation—essential for personal and collective survival in any era. They remind us that while the context may change, the core challenges of human existence remain constant.

This chapter will delve into specific myths that exemplify how ancient wisdom can be applied to modern issues such as leadership, justice, and personal growth. Through these stories, we'll uncover enduring strategies for navigating life's complexities—a testament to the timeless nature of these ancient narratives.

By revisiting these ancient tales with fresh eyes, we pay homage to a rich cultural heritage and enrich our understanding of ourselves and our society. Egyptian mythology holds keys to understanding universal truths about human nature that are often overlooked in contemporary discourse.

As we move forward in this exploration, remember that the value of mythology lies not in its age but in its ability to speak truths across centuries. Let us embrace these old yet ever-new stories with an open mind, ready to learn from our ancestors who faced many of the same fears and hopes that define human life today.

This journey through Egyptian mythology is more than an academic exercise; it is an invitation to weave ancient wisdom into the fabric of our daily lives. Doing so ensures that these timeless tales continue to enlighten and inspire future generations.

Misconceptions Around Egyptian Mythology

One common misconception about Egyptian mythology is that it needs to be more ancient to be relevant today. Think of Egyptian mythology as a tool, not unlike a hammer. Just as a hammer was used thousands of years ago and is still valid today, the themes and lessons from Egyptian myths hold valuable insights for contemporary life.

Egyptian mythology is often seen as complex and filled with strange gods and bizarre tales. However, this complexity mirrors the rich tapestry of human emotion and experience. These stories are not just about gods and magic but about fundamental human experiences—love, betrayal, ambition, and fear.

Another misconception is that these myths are purely religious or historical, relevant only in academic or theological contexts. This is like assuming Shakespeare's plays are only for actors and literature professors. In reality, both Shakespeare's works and Egyptian myths delve into the essence of human nature, exploring themes that resonate personally with anyone.

Many dismiss these myths as irrelevant because they need to see the immediate application in the fast-paced digital age. Yet, just as a map of an ancient city can give us insight into its history and influence its modern layout, Egyptian myths provide a map of human psychology that remains pertinent.

In essence, dismissing Egyptian mythology as irrelevant means overlooking the universal and timeless human stories it encapsulates.

Universal Emotions in Mythological Themes

Egyptian myths, rich with stories of gods and pharaohs, fundamentally explore universal human emotions. Take the myth of Isis and Osiris, for example, a profound tale of love, jealousy, death, and redemption. These are feelings and experiences that every person encounters in their life.

Why do these ancient stories still tug at our hearts and stir our imaginations? They reflect our own lives, struggles, joys, and vulnerabilities. When Osiris is betrayed and dismembered, isn't that a reflection of our own experiences of betrayal and loss? When Isis searches tirelessly for Osiris, does it not echo our quests for healing and wholeness?

Consider the myth of Horus, a tale of rightful authority and personal growth. This story mirrors the journey many of us undertake to establish our identity and assert our place in the world. Horus's battles symbolize the challenges in our careers or personal development.

The emotional depth in these myths is not just historical; it's deeply woven into the fabric of everyday life. By understanding the emotional core of these stories, we can better understand ourselves and the people around us.

Could recognizing our reflections in these ancient mirrors reveal insights into our lives?

Modern Relevance of Ancient Wisdom

In our modern world, full of rapid change and uncertainty, the ancient myths of Egypt are more relevant than ever. They offer a way to understand and navigate personal and societal upheavals. Consider the myth of Ma'at, the goddess of truth, balance, and order. In times of social or personal turmoil, striving for Ma'at's ideals can guide us toward harmony and stability.

These myths also offer a framework for resilience. The story of Set, the god of chaos and disorder, teaches that disruption and difficulty are part of the human condition. Yet, the narrative does not end with chaos but shows us the potential for overcoming adversity through strength and determination.

Imagine a community facing a natural disaster. The cooperative and strategic efforts required for recovery are not unlike those of the gods and heroes in Egyptian myths. These stories can inspire and motivate us to act with courage and unity.

Moreover, these myths provide a moral compass. They teach values such as justice, courage, and wisdom, indispensable in dealing with contemporary ethical dilemmas. Whether it's navigating a difficult personal decision or addressing global issues like inequality or environmental crisis, the lessons from these ancient stories remain profoundly relevant.

The timeless nature of Egyptian myths makes them invaluable tools for understanding the past and navigating the complexities of the present and future.

In this chapter, we've delved into the rich tapestry of Egyptian mythology, uncovering the depth and relevance of these ancient stories to our modern lives. Far from being mere relics of the past, these myths offer **profound insights** into the human condition, reflecting universal emotions and experiences that resonate deeply with us today.

We began by addressing **common misconceptions** that often paint these narratives as irrelevant or arcane. By peeling back layers of misunderstanding, we revealed how these myths are not just about gods and pharaohs but are stories steeped in the everyday struggles and triumphs familiar to us all. This recognition invites us to look beyond the surface and appreciate the enduring wisdom embedded in these ancient tales.

Through the stories of Isis' perseverance, Osiris' resurrection, and Horus' quest for justice, we connect with fundamental human themes of love, loss, and redemption. These narratives remind us that the challenges we face today are not so different from those encountered by our ancestors. The emotional core of these myths helps us feel less isolated in our struggles, providing a sense of continuity and resilience that is both comforting and empowering.

Moreover, these ancient myths can serve as **beacons of stability and hope** in times of personal and societal upheaval. They teach us about endurance and adaptation, showing how to navigate the complexities of life with courage and wisdom. We can tackle modern challenges with a renewed perspective and a stronger sense of purpose by applying these age-old lessons.

Let us carry forward the wisdom of the ancients, not as distant and dusty relics but as living, breathing sources of inspiration that guide us in navigating our complex world. Embracing these stories can transform our understanding of ourselves and society, encouraging us to live more thoughtfully and boldly.

As we move forward in this book, remember the power of mythology to illuminate paths during dark times and to foster a deeper connection with the timeless human spirit. By integrating these ancient lessons into our lives, we honor our past and enrich our present and future with a renewed sense of possibility and hope.

Chapter 3: Divine Symbols: Decoding The Nature and Virtue in Egyptian Deities

In the dim light of early morning, Cairo's bustling streets began to stir as Mariam stepped out from her modest apartment. The air was crisp, carrying the scent of the Nile that meandered through the ancient city, whispering secrets of ages past. Today was not just another day for Mariam; it was a day she hoped would bring clarity to her restless spirit.

She walked purposefully toward the Museum of Egyptian Antiquities, her place of work and sanctuary. As an archivist, Mariam had spent countless hours among relics and manuscripts, each telling tales of gods and mortals intertwined in an eternal dance. Yet today, her thoughts were occupied by three particular deities: Osiris, Isis, and Horus. Their stories were not merely myths to her but reflections of life's profound truths.

Inside the museum's cool stone walls, Mariam moved towards an exhibit that housed a beautifully inscribed sarcophagus depicting Osiris. The god of the afterlife stood regal and serene, his green skin symbolizing rebirth and renewal. As she gazed at his figure, Mariam felt a connection to the cycles in her own life—the losses she had endured and the new beginnings that had surprisingly sprouted from her deepest sorrows.

A few steps away, the figure of Isis with outstretched wings caught her eye. The goddess's determination to resurrect Osiris spoke volumes about devotion and enduring love. Mariam recalled her grandmother's tales of how Isis exemplified strength and healing. She pondered on her relationships—how often had she summoned such strength? How frequently had she been a source of healing?

Her thoughts were interrupted by the chatter of a group of schoolchildren crowding around the statue of Horus. His falcon head symbolized protection and watchfulness over Egypt; his eye represented healing and restoration. Observing their curious eyes and eager faces,

Mariam smiled softly. Horus's symbolism reminded her that vigilance and protection were not confined to grand gestures but found in everyday acts—watching over a younger sibling or caring for an aging neighbor.

As she moved through the exhibits with soft steps echoing slightly on marble floors, each artifact whispered bits of wisdom about nature's forces mirrored in human virtues—about how understanding these could enrich one's self-awareness.

Outside again, under Cairo's broad sky, turning brighter with each passing minute, Marian felt enriched yet burdened by new insights into divine-human connections through these ancient deities. She wondered how this deeper understanding might influence personal introspection and interpersonal dynamics within communities.

These communities, bound by modern complexities rooted in ancient lands, face issues that have deep historical roots, and understanding these roots can help us navigate these challenges.

Could recognizing oneself in these age-old symbols foster more profound empathy? By understanding the struggles and triumphs of these ancient deities, we can develop a deeper empathy for the human experience, both past and present. This empathy can help us relate to others and understand their journeys, fostering stronger connections and a more compassionate society.

Unveiling the Timeless Wisdom of Egyptian Deities

With its rich tapestry of gods and goddesses, Egyptian mythology has fascinated scholars and spiritual seekers for centuries. This ancient pantheon is not merely a collection of stories but a profound embodiment of natural forces and human virtues. By exploring the symbols represented by key deities such as Osiris, Isis, and Horus, we can uncover insights about our nature and the universe around us that are as relevant today as they were in ancient *times*.

At the heart of these mythologies lie profound truths about existence, relationships, and personal growth. The gods of Egypt teach us about the cycles of life and death, the importance of balance and justice, and the power of resurrection. These themes are not just historical curiosities—they are vibrant, living concepts that can still inform our lives today.

Reflecting on Our Inner Nature Through Osiris and Isis

Osiris, often associated with regeneration and rebirth, symbolizes more than just physical renewal. He represents a continual process of inner transformation that we can undergo. Understanding Osiris helps us see every ending in our lives as a potential beginning and every loss as an opportunity for profound personal growth.

Isis, his consort, embodies the virtues of devotion and healing. Her legendary love for Osiris and her quest to restore him teaches us about the power of faith and perseverance in overcoming despair.

Reflecting on Isis's story teaches us how to heal ourselves and extend this healing to others.

Horus: A Symbol of Power and Protection

Horus, the son of Isis and Osiris, brings another dimension to our understanding of Egyptian deities. He is often depicted as a falcon overseeing the land, representing light and goodness. Horus's vigilant eye reminds us that we can protect what is valuable—our personal integrity or our natural environment.

Interpersonal Relationships Enhanced by Mythological Insights

The dynamics among these deities also offer rich lessons in handling relationships. The conflicts and resolutions seen in their stories mirror our own interpersonal struggles. By studying these divine narratives, we gain insight into resolving conflicts, fostering forgiveness, and building enduring bonds with those around us.

Understanding these ancient symbols encourages a deeper connection with ourselves and the world at large. It prompts us to consider how ancient wisdom can be applied to modern challenges—encouraging sustainability, promoting peace, and enhancing personal well-being. By applying these insights, we can actively shape our lives and the world around us.

As we delve deeper into each deity's attributes in subsequent sections, remember that these figures are more than mythological characters; they are mirrors reflecting our own humanity back at us.

By embracing their wisdom and interpreting it in our own lives, we can transform how we interact with our world and each other.

Your active engagement in this process is key to unlocking the full potential of these ancient teachings.

Exploring Egyptian Deities: Osiris, Isis, and Horus

Egyptian mythology is rich with symbols and characters that extend beyond simple storytelling. Among the most significant are Osiris, Isis, and Horus. Osiris, often depicted as a green-skinned deity, represents regeneration and resurrection. His story tells of betrayal and rebirth, mirroring the agricultural cycle of sowing and harvesting.

Imagine a tree that falls, only to have its seeds sprout new life. This is the essence of Osiris — a symbol of life springing from death. Isis, his consort, embodies healing and protection. She is often shown with wings, encompassing her role as a guardian. Her tales of unwavering loyalty and magical prowess serve as a beacon of hope and a protective figure.

Horus, the falcon-headed god, symbolizes kingship and the sky. His right eye represents the sun, and his left is the moon, reflecting his domain over the heavens. The myth of Horus battling Set, his uncle, emphasizes the theme of rightful rule and order overcoming chaos.

Each deity tells a part of the Egyptian spiritual narrative and offers insights into natural cycles and human characteristics. *Osiris, Isis, and Horus embody life, protection, and leadership.*

The Representation of Natural Forces and Human Virtues

These deities are not mere characters but profound representations of the natural world and human virtues. Osiris's connection to vegetation and rebirth mirrors Earth's natural cycle of life and renewal. This cycle is fundamental to our understanding of sustainability and ecological balance.

Isis's role as a healer and protector can be likened to the nurturing aspect of nature and the care humans must take in preserving their surroundings and supporting each other. Her magical skills emphasize the power of knowledge and wisdom in overcoming difficulties.

Horus's depiction as a sky god involves more than the literal heavens; it symbolizes human nature's vast potential and ambition.

His narrative with Set highlights the eternal struggle between order and chaos, a balance necessary for the prosperity of any society.

Through these myths, ancient Egyptians expressed deep understandings of the world around them and their place within it.

Can recognizing these symbols in our lives today lead to a deeper appreciation of our natural world and personal virtues?

Impact on Self-Awareness and Interpersonal Relationships

Understanding these symbols fosters greater self-awareness. By seeing Osiris in the cycles of our own lives, we might better accept changes and endings as precursors to new beginnings. Recognizing Isis in our interactions reminds us of the importance of empathy and protection in our relationships.

Horus teaches us the importance of leadership and the vision required to maintain balance. His struggles and victories encourage us to strive for harmony in our personal and professional endeavors.

Such insights deepen our understanding of ourselves and enhance our interactions with others. They teach us the value of resilience, care, and foresight in nurturing healthy relationships and communities.

By examining these ancient symbols, we connect more deeply with ourselves and each other, meaningfully bridging the past and present.

Reflecting on the profound narratives of Osiris, Isis, and Horus, we uncover not just stories of divine beings but a mirror reflecting our own nature and the world around us. These deities, emblematic of elements like life, death, magic, and protection, invite us to explore the depth of our virtues and the forces that shape our existence.

Understanding these symbols deepens our self-awareness.

Recognizing Osiris in our resilience, Isis in our wisdom, and Horus in our capacity for renewal, we learn to navigate life's complexities with greater clarity and purpose. This awareness is not an academic exercise but a transformative experience that enhances how we view ourselves and interact with others.

Moreover, embracing these ancient symbols fosters stronger connections with those around us. The virtues represented by these deities—justice, perseverance, healing—are universal, transcending time and culture. By recognizing these qualities within ourselves and others, we bridge divides and build more empathetic and understanding relationships.

These insights do not merely enrich our personal lives; they also encourage us to engage more harmoniously with the world. As we align more closely with the natural forces symbolized by Egyptian deities, we become more attuned to the environment and the larger forces at play in our lives.

Let us carry forward the wisdom of the ancients not as distant myths but as living truths that continue to shape our modern existence. By integrating these timeless lessons into our daily lives, we honor our past and enrich our future, fostering a life of greater harmony and understanding.

In embracing Egyptian mythology's wisdom, we find a link to an ancient past and timeless guidance for living well in the present. Let this knowledge inspire us to lead lives marked by more profound wisdom, connection, and fulfillment.

Chapter 4: Mythology Made Easy: Accessible Approaches to Ancient Stories

In the muted light of a Cairo library, the dust danced like tiny golden pharaohs in the slanted sunbeams. Sarah, an earnest historian interested in Egyptian mythology, stood amidst towering shelves that held whispers of ancient secrets. Her fingers trailed over the spines of books as if touching the very backbone of history itself.

She pulled out a thick volume, its cover embossed with the intricate depiction of Anubis, the god of mummification and the afterlife.

Today was not just another day; it was the beginning of her mission to demystify the complexities of Egyptian myths for her upcoming lecture series aimed at young scholars. The challenge loomed in her mind—how to simplify these tangled tales laden with gods and magic into digestible, engaging stories?

As she flipped through the pages, her mind wandered to her first encounter with the myth of Osiris and Isis. It had been in this very library, under this very dome, where sunlight now painted patterns on old wood. She remembered how the story had seemed enchanting and overwhelming—a tapestry too intricate to unravel.

Her reverie was broken by a soft cough from Mrs. Hafez, the librarian, who approached with a smile that seemed both knowing and encouraging. *"Finding what you need, Sarah?"*

"Yes and no," Sarah replied, intending to break down these myths for easier consumption. *"It's about making them accessible without losing their essence."*

Mrs. Hafez nodded sagely as she adjusted her glasses. *"Perhaps focus on one deity or myth at a time? Build up from there."*

Encouraged by Mrs. Hafez's simple yet profound suggestion, Sarah felt a renewed sense of purpose. She decided to start with Anubis—his role was crucial yet finite enough to encapsulate in a single lecture.

The clock ticked away as Sarah gathered books and notes around her like building blocks for her intellectual construction project. Each book opened paths that delved deep into rituals and symbols and branched into human emotions and cultural values resonating across millennia.

As she absorbed herself in research, deciphering hieroglyphs that seemed as complex as constellations, she couldn't help but feel connected to those ancient scribes whose hands had once painted these sacred texts.

The sun dipped lower, casting long shadows across Sarah's table, which was strewn with notes and books. The day was ending, but her journey into simplifying these myths had just begun.

How will understanding Anubis help unlock other elements of Egyptian mythology for Sarah's students?

Unlocking the Mysteries: Simplifying the Complex World of Egyptian Mythology

With its intricate web of gods and goddesses, epic tales, and symbolic rituals, Egyptian mythology often appears as a labyrinthine treasure trove that only scholars could navigate. Yet, the essence of these ancient stories holds profound relevance even in our modern lives. The challenge lies not in the value of these myths but in their accessibility. Many potential learners feel daunted by the complexity and richness of this ancient narrative landscape. This chapter aims to bridge that gap, offering practical strategies to make Egyptian mythology approachable and engaging for everyone.

Making Learning Manageable

The first step in demystifying Egyptian mythology is breaking it down into manageable parts. Learners can gradually build a comprehensive understanding without feeling overwhelmed by focusing on individual myths or specific deities. This approach simplifies learning and allows for deeper engagement with each element of the mythology.

Through this systematic exploration, each myth and god becomes a piece of a larger puzzle that learners can assemble at their own pace.

Focused Topics for Deep Dive

Delving into focused topics one at a time enriches comprehension and retains interest. Instead of trying to grasp Egyptian religious practices or the full pantheon of gods at once, learners can explore one deity or mythological event in detail. This deep-dive approach helps form clearer connections and insights, making the learning process both enjoyable and informative.

Enjoyment in Education

The joy of learning about Egyptian mythology should be considered. Techniques that make education enjoyable are crucial in sustaining interest and motivation. Integrating storytelling methods, interactive discussions, and creative interpretations can transform a seemingly dry historical study into an exciting adventure. We invite continuous curiosity and deeper exploration by making the learning process fun.

The overarching theme of this book emphasizes how ancient wisdom can be integrated into modern life. Understanding Egyptian mythology through simplified, accessible methods enlightens and empowers individuals by connecting them with timeless narratives that reflect human experiences and emotions throughout history.

As we navigate these strategies in this chapter, we will see how demystifying complex information enriches understanding and appreciation. The goal is to ensure that every reader comes away with a robust toolkit for tackling what once seemed an impossible body of knowledge.

Through reflective anecdotes and thoughtful insights, this chapter will guide you through the historical complexities and show how these ancient myths can offer valuable lessons applicable to contemporary challenges. By reducing barriers to understanding and enhancing accessibility, we open up a world where every reader can find value and inspiration in the tales of ancient Egypt.

Join us as we unfold these narratives with clarity and enthusiasm.

We aim to transform daunting complexity into inviting clarity, making ancient Egyptian mythology not just learned but truly lived.

Simplifying Complex Egyptian Myths

With their elaborate stories and numerous deities, Egyptian myths can initially seem like a labyrinthine tapestry to the untrained eye.

The key to unraveling this complexity is breaking down the myths into manageable themes. By identifying core elements—like creation, death, or resurrection—learners can begin to see patterns and connections between different myths.

Consider the myth of Osiris, for instance. It's a story about betrayal, death, and the triumphant return to life, themes that resonate universally. By focusing on these fundamental aspects, the myth becomes not just a series of events in a distant culture but a narrative with emotional depth and universal appeal.

Approaching these stories by themes rather than trying to digest entire myths in one go makes the learning process more manageable. It's similar to assembling a puzzle; start with the corner pieces and slowly fill in the center as the picture becomes more apparent.

Imagine you're learning to cook a complex dish. You would only start with some of the ingredients at a time. Instead, you'd tackle one part of the recipe at a time. Similarly, dissecting myths into themes allows for a step-by-step approach that builds a comprehensive understanding without overwhelming the learner.

Simplifying mythology into core themes makes the learning journey accessible and engaging.

Exploring Individual Topics for Depth

When learning about Egyptian mythology, diving deep into individual topics can significantly enhance understanding. Take, for instance, the god Thoth, the deity of wisdom and writing.

Studying Thoth involves not only learning his characteristics and stories but also exploring his influence on Egyptian culture and religion.

Incorporating various sources, such as historical texts, archaeological findings, and expert interpretations, can provide a well-rounded view of Thoth. This method allows learners to appreciate the depth of his role and the nuances of his interactions with other deities.

Consider each myth or deity using analogies like a book in a vast library. Just as you might explore a favorite author by reading all their works, studying one god or myth in detail can open up a richer, more detailed understanding of the mythological world.

By focusing on one deity at a time, learners can form connections between the mythology and its cultural context, seeing how these stories influenced Egyptian thought, art, and daily life. This focused approach not only makes learning more manageable but also more meaningful.

Could delving deeper into one myth or deity at a time be the key to unlocking the mysteries of Egyptian mythology?

Making Mythology Enjoyable and Accessible

Learning about mythology should be an enjoyable experience, a manageable task. Incorporating interactive elements such as storytelling sessions, visual aids like maps and diagrams, and even quizzes can make the process more engaging.

Think of mythology as a grand theater play, where every story is a scene and every deity a character. Presenting myths in a dynamic and entertaining format makes learners more likely to engage with the material and retain information.

Discussing myths in groups can also enhance enjoyment, as it allows for the sharing of ideas and perspectives. This social aspect of learning can make complex topics more accessible and less intimidating.

Educators can use simple language and clear explanations to ensure that learners are not bogged down by complex terminology or convoluted narratives. This approach helps to maintain interest and encourages deeper exploration.

Integrating interactive elements, focusing on enjoyment, and using precise language is crucial in making Egyptian mythology accessible and engaging for all learners.

By simplifying myths into themes, exploring each topic in depth, and making the learning process enjoyable, we can demystify the complex world of Egyptian mythology, making it accessible and engaging for everyone.

Understanding Egyptian mythology can often feel like deciphering a complex tapestry woven with intricate patterns of gods, myths, and ancient lore. However, by adopting simplified learning approaches, we can demystify these narratives, making them not only accessible but also deeply enriching.

Step-by-Step Guide: Unraveling the Threads of Time

The journey into Egyptian mythology begins with *choosing a specific myth or theme* that sparks your curiosity. Whether it's the epic tale of Isis and Osiris or the celestial journey of Amun-Ra, selecting a focal point simplifies the entry into this vast mythological field.

Once a theme is chosen, the next step is to *break down the myth* into digestible segments. Identifying key characters, pivotal events, and symbolic elements helps understand the myth's core messages.

This segmentation transforms a sprawling narrative into manageable insights that are easier to explore and appreciate.

The third phase involves *research and information gathering*.

Delve into various sources—books, scholarly articles, and even multimedia presentations—to gather diverse perspectives on the chosen theme. This enriches your understanding and provides a multi-dimensional view of the mythology.

Following research, *analyze and interpret* the information. Reflect on how the symbolism and moral lessons relate to the ancient world and contemporary life. This step bridges the gap between past wisdom and modern experiences, highlighting the relevance of these ancient stories today.

To deepen your engagement with Egyptian mythology, *participate in discussions and reflections* with others who share your interest. This could be in online forums, book clubs, or study groups.

Sharing interpretations and listening to others enriches your perspective and enhances your understanding.

The penultimate step is to *apply the lessons learned* to your own life. Ancient myths, despite their age, contain timeless wisdom that can offer guidance and insight into personal and professional challenges faced in the modern world.

Finally, *repeat this process* with new myths or themes. Each story offers unique insights and adds layers to your understanding of Egyptian mythology. This ongoing journey builds your knowledge and connects you to the rich spiritual heritage of ancient Egypt.

By following these steps, you gradually peel away the layers of complexity surrounding Egyptian mythology. This systematic exploration allows you to appreciate its richness and depth without feeling overwhelmed. It transforms what could be an arduous task into an enjoyable and fulfilling journey of discovery. Embrace these stories from the past to enrich your understanding of the world today, and let them guide you in navigating contemporary issues with ancient wisdom.

Chapter 5: Timeless Lessons: Applying Ancient Wisdom to Modern Dilemmas

In the dim light of early morning, Thomas walked through the damp streets of a small English village, his footsteps echoing off the cobblestones and his breath forming clouds in the chill air. He had always found solace in these solitary walks, a time to wrestle with the constant problems that crowded his mind. Today was no different, but the nature of his plight had shifted from the mundane to the mythical.

Thomas, a middle-aged professor of ancient history, was deeply immersed in preparing a lecture series on Egyptian mythology and its relevance to modern-day ethics. The story of Isis and Osiris particularly haunted him—not just as a tale of gods and betrayal but as a mirror reflecting his recent turmoil in personal relationships and career paths.

As he passed by the closed shops with their darkened windows reflecting back his thoughtful gaze, Thomas pondered over Isis' unyielding search for her husband Osiris after he was betrayed and killed by Set. Her dedication spoke to him of loyalty and resilience—qualities he feared were becoming obsolete in contemporary professional relationships. Could one still afford such loyalty without being exploited?

The crisp morning air carried whispers of awakening as doors began to open and people started their day's labor. A young woman arranging flowers outside her shop caught Thomas' eye. She worked with such meticulous care that each bloom seemed to stand out vividly against its neighbors—a symphony of color that drew passersby into her small universe.

This image struck Thomas profoundly; wasn't this what Isis did? In piecing together Osiris' scattered remains, she focused on each fragment and detail with immense care, ultimately bringing about resurrection and new life. In his own life, could Thomas apply this principle to mend fragmented professional relationships or revive stalled projects?

His thoughts were momentarily interrupted by a dog straining at its leash towards him, its tail wagging energetically despite its owner's reprimand. It reminded him that life was persistent and often messy—an interplay of various forces that sometimes required one to be resilient like Isis and adaptable like Osiris, who became lord of the underworld.

As he turned towards home, Thomas felt a mixture of trepidation and resolve stir within him. Today's lecture would be more than an academic exercise; it would explore how ancient wisdom could be applied to contemporary moral dilemmas about loyalty, loss, ambition, and recovery.

Let's learn from Isis' example of how to repair what is broken and reinvent ourselves amidst our scattered pieces.

Unveiling Timeless Wisdom: How Ancient Egyptian Myths Illuminate Today's Challenges

The wisdom of the ancients is not just a relic of the past but a living, breathing guide that can help us navigate the complexities of modern life. This chapter delves into the rich tapestry of ancient Egyptian mythology, drawing parallels between historical narratives and contemporary dilemmas to offer practical guidance for our personal and professional lives. Through a detailed exploration of themes such as justice, loyalty, and resilience, we uncover the enduring relevance of these age-old stories.

Ancient Egypt's myths are more than just tales of gods and pharaohs; they encapsulate fundamental human experiences and ethical quandaries that resonate deeply with today's societal issues. By comparing these ancient moral dilemmas with those we face in the 21st century, we can extract lessons that are surprisingly applicable to our current circumstances. This analysis enriches our understanding of Egyptian culture. It provides us with a unique lens through which to view our challenges.

We will explore how these myths can provide *practical guidance for navigating personal relationships* and career transitions. For example, the story of Isis and Osiris offers profound insights into themes of love, loss, and rebirth—themes that are universally relevant and can be particularly poignant during times of personal change or hardship. By interpreting these myths through a modern lens, we gain access to a wealth of wisdom to help us manage complex emotions and make difficult decisions.

Reflecting on Personal Growth Through Ancient Narratives

Egyptian mythology's emotional depth and moral complexity can be a powerful tool for self-reflection and personal growth. As we dissect the choices and consequences faced by figures like Isis and Osiris, we are prompted to examine our values and behaviors in a new light. This introspective journey enhances our self-awareness and empowers us to take more mindful actions in our daily lives.

Applying Mythological Insights to Professional Challenges

In addition to personal development, ancient myths offer invaluable professional conduct and ethics perspectives. The strategic maneuvers and leadership qualities exhibited by deities and heroes in these stories can inspire contemporary professionals to adopt more innovative and ethical approaches to their work. Readers can glean strategies applicable in modern business environments by analyzing how legendary characters navigated trials and achieved their goals.

This chapter aims to educate and inspire by demonstrating how ancient wisdom can be effectively applied to solve modern problems. Whether you are dealing with workplace dynamics, personal relationships, or existential questions about your life's direction, the lessons drawn from Egyptian mythology can provide clarity and direction.

In embracing these timeless narratives, we reconnect with a part of human history that still holds significant power today. As we forge ahead in our fast-paced world, let us take a moment to look back at the ancients—not just for knowledge but for inspiration and guidance on our path forward.

In ancient Egyptian mythology, the moral dilemmas and themes often mirrored the complexities of human nature and the societal interactions we experience today. Looking closely, we see that stories like that of Ma'at, the goddess of truth and justice, resonate deeply with our contemporary struggles for fairness and ethical integrity. Ma'at's principle that everyone—regardless of status—should be judged by their actions is a timeless notion, underscoring accountability's importance in ancient and modern governance.

The analogy of Ma'at's feather, against which the hearts of the deceased were weighed, serves as a symbolic compass for today's ethical decision-making. As a heart burdened with misdeeds tips the scales towards chaos, so does unethical behavior disrupt modern society. This visual provides a straightforward yet profound way to reflect on the impact of our actions, encouraging a balanced approach to personal and professional challenges.

Similarly, the myth of Horus and Seth, which deals with rightful leadership and the power struggle, mirrors modern-day corporate battles and political campaigns. The chaotic and often aggressive rivalry between Horus, the legitimate ruler, and his uncle Seth, the usurper, can be likened to contemporary conflicts over leadership in organizations and countries. This story teaches the value of perseverance and legitimacy, advocating for rightful leadership and the resolution of disputes through wisdom and justice.

In daily life, these ancient narratives encourage reflection on our actions and their repercussions on our community and workplace.

By aligning our behavior with Ma'at's principles of truth and justice, we ensure a harmonious social and professional environment and foster a culture of integrity and respect. This reflection on ancient ethics offers practical guidance for navigating today's complex moral landscape.

In essence, the moral dilemmas of ancient Egypt are not relics of the past but are vibrantly relevant, offering clear guidance for contemporary ethical conduct.

Extracting Modern Wisdom from Mythical Narratives

Ancient myths, rich with complex characters and dramatic plots, provide more than just entertainment; they offer a treasure trove of wisdom applicable to personal and professional growth. Consider the story of Thoth, the god of wisdom, who mediated disputes among gods with his vast knowledge. This myth underscores the importance of diplomacy and learning in resolving conflicts—an essential skill in any professional setting where negotiation and conflict resolution are daily occurrences.

Thoth's role as a mediator teaches the value of knowledge and tact over brute force. In modern workplaces, this translates to the importance of informed decision-making and gracefully navigating complex human dynamics. Just as Thoth used wisdom to calm stormy waters, modern leaders can use their knowledge and skills to guide their teams through challenges.

By delving into these stories, we unearth layers of meaning that inform our understanding of human behavior and motivations. This exploration deepens our ability to empathize with others, a crucial skill in personal relationships and professional teamwork. The myth of Thoth does not just belong to the past; it lives on through the lessons it imparts about the power of wisdom and diplomacy.

Can the wisdom of Thoth help you rethink your approach to the conflicts and challenges in your life?

Understanding Isis and Osiris: Lessons for Today

One of the most poignant myths of ancient Egypt, the tale of Isis and Osiris, offers rich insights into the themes of love, loss, and resilience. Osiris, the god of the underworld whose life and death symbolize the cycles of nature, teaches us about the inevitability of change and the importance of adaptation—a lesson highly relevant to both personal relationships and career transitions.

Step 1: Identify and Break Down the Myth

Identifying the story of Isis and Osiris involves understanding the characters—Isis, the devoted wife; Osiris, the benevolent ruler; and Set, the embodiment of jealousy and chaos. Analyzing these roles sheds light on the dynamics of human relationships and the impacts of external forces on these relationships.

Step 2: Analyze Components and Values

The next step is to delve into the values and principles depicted in the myth. Loyalty, perseverance, and renewal emerge as central themes, reflecting the enduring struggle against adversity and the potential for rebirth and new beginnings.

Step 3: Relate to Contemporary Issues

We can draw parallels that provide comfort and guidance by relating these ancient themes to modern-day challenges, such as a career change or the loss of a loved one. For instance, just as Isis reassembled Osiris, we, too, can gather the fragmented pieces of our past experiences to reconstruct a coherent path forward.

Step 4: Formulate Actionable Strategies

The final step is to transform these insights into actionable strategies. This might involve embracing change and viewing setbacks as opportunities for growth, much like Osiris's transformation into the god of the underworld symbolizes a new beginning.

By following this framework, we can apply the lessons from the myth of Isis and Osiris to our contemporary dilemmas, finding resilience and renewal in our lives.

Throughout this exploration of ancient Egyptian wisdom, we've unearthed valuable insights that resonate deeply with today's challenges and decisions. By drawing parallels between the moral dilemmas of the past and those of today, it becomes evident that human nature and the struggles we encounter have remained mainly consistent throughout the ages.

The relevance of these age-old stories is profound. Reflecting on the narrative of Isis and Osiris, for instance, we gain perspectives on resilience and renewal that apply to personal relationships and career transitions. Their tale, emphasizing themes such as love, loss, and rebirth, is a powerful reminder of our capacity to overcome adversity and emerge stronger.

What strikes a chord is not just the similarity of issues then and now but also how these myths offer ***practical guidance.*** For anyone navigating the complexities of modern relationships or facing pivotal career decisions, these stories act as a compass, guiding us with principles that have stood the test of time. They encourage us to persevere, rebuild, and reinvent ourselves when faced with life's inevitable upheavals.

Moreover, engaging with these stories enriches our understanding of human emotions and motivations, enhancing our empathy and ability to navigate diverse social landscapes. It's a testament to the enduring power of storytelling and its capacity to inspire and instruct across millennia.

Let us carry forward this ancient wisdom, allowing it to illuminate paths in our own journeys. Whether facing new beginnings, confronting setbacks, or seeking fulfillment, the lessons encapsulated in these myths provide a beacon. They remind us that, though times change, the essence of human experience remains the same—rich with challenges but also opportunities for growth and transformation.

By embracing this timeless wisdom, we not only solve our own modern dilemmas but also connect more deeply with a shared human heritage that continues to inspire, comfort, and guide us through the complexities of contemporary life. Let these stories be both a mirror reflecting our own lives and a map leading us toward greater understanding and resilience.

Chapter 6: Inner Mirrors: Reflecting on Mythology for Personal Growth

Elena stood by the window, the early morning light casting long shadows across her small, cluttered study floor. She gazed out at the bustling street below, her mind a whirlwind of ancient symbols and mythological motifs. Today, like every day, she planned to delve deeper into her understanding of Egyptian mythology, attempting to weave its rich narratives into the fabric of her everyday life.

She turned from the window and picked up an old leather-bound journal from her desk. Its pages were filled with handwritten notes on Osiris, Isis, and other deities—gods who had mastered the art of dying and rebirth long before modern tales tried to echo their depth. As she flipped through the pages, Elena reflected on how these stories mirrored her experiences with loss and renewal. Her father's passing last year had plunged her into a deep sorrow from which she was only beginning to emerge.

Sitting down at her desk, Elena began to write. She wrote about how Isis's search for Osiris's scattered pieces across Egypt reminded her of piecing together her fragmented self in the aftermath of grief. The pen moved fluidly across the paper as if drawing strength from some ancient wellspring of wisdom.

A knock on the door interrupted her flow. Mrs. Henderson from next door was holding a tray with two cups of tea. Elena welcomed the interruption and the company. They sat together, sipping tea as Mrs. Henderson discussed community matters and local events.

After Mrs. Henderson left, Elena returned to her journaling. Still, she was distracted by thoughts of integrating these mythological lessons into public aspects of her life. She could start a community group or workshop where these ancient stories could be discussed and applied in modern contexts. The idea felt daunting yet invigorating.

As dusk fell over the city and painted Elena's study in shades of grey and gold, she paused and looked again at those scattered notes around her desk—their edges now glowing in the low light. How could these old myths help herself and others navigate their personal trials? Could shared reflection lead them all toward deeper understanding?

Elena closed her eyes briefly, then opened them with renewed purpose as she stared back down at an open page before her—her pen poised to capture another revelation that bridged the past with the present. What lessons do we carry forward from our ancestors that are still relevant today?

Discover Your Reflection in the Sands of Time

In our fast-paced modern world, it can be easy to feel disconnected from the deeper currents that have shaped human consciousness for millennia. Yet, buried within the vast narratives of Egyptian mythology, timeless lessons are waiting to be unearthed that can profoundly influence our personal growth and day-to-day life. This exploration into the reflective practices centered around these ancient stories offers a unique opportunity to understand ourselves better and integrate this age-old wisdom into our contemporary existence.

Reflective practices such as ***journaling*** and ***discussion*** are powerful tools for personal development. By engaging with these methods, individuals can delve deeper into the mythological themes presented by Egyptian lore, uncovering parallels between these tales and their own life experiences. This process enriches one's understanding and fosters a greater connection with a cultural heritage that has long influenced human thought and philosophy.

Egyptian mythology provides a particularly fertile ground for reflection with its rich tapestry of gods, goddesses, and symbolic narratives. These stories are not just historical relics but are imbued with psychological insights and existential questions that are still relevant today. Individuals can gain new perspectives on their challenges and achievements by identifying personal experiences that resonate with these ancient themes.

Moreover, discussing how to integrate mythological lessons into everyday life is crucial for applying this wisdom. It's one thing to read and appreciate a story's moral; it's another to live out its lessons in the context of modern stresses and decisions. This chapter will explore various methods by which these age-old truths can be woven into the fabric of our daily lives, enhancing personal fulfillment and emotional resilience.

The journey through Egyptian mythology is akin to looking into a mirror that reflects our individual identities and our collective human heritage. By engaging in reflective practices connecting us with these ancient narratives, we open ourselves to profound insights and transformative experiences. This chapter invites readers to embark on this introspective journey, promising them not just knowledge of a distant past but a renewed understanding of their place in today's world.

In embracing these reflective practices, we honor our ancestors' wisdom and empower ourselves to lead more mindful and meaningful lives. The stories of gods and pharaohs, so seemingly distant, illuminate paths in our journeys, guiding us through challenges and inspiring us toward self-discovery and growth.

Thus begins our exploration of how ancient Egyptian wisdom can be mirrored in our modern lives—an endeavor that promises both enlightenment and inspiration.

Reflective practices such as journaling and engaging in thoughtful discussions provide a powerful avenue for deepening one's understanding of mythological themes. By regularly writing down thoughts and perceptions about these ancient stories, individuals can uncover new layers of meaning and personal relevance. Journaling acts as a mirror, reflecting the internal landscape and allowing one to see how mythological themes like transformation, resilience, and rebirth are echoed in their own life experiences.

Imagine planting a seed in fertile soil. Just as the seed needs water, sunlight, and time to grow, understanding mythological themes requires nurturance through reflection and patience. Journaling is the sunlight, discussions are the water and time spent in contemplation is the fertile soil that brings forth the rich insights from the depths of these ancient stories.

Discussing these themes with others can also significantly amplify personal insights. Conversations open up new perspectives and challenge one's own interpretations, much like how different climates affect plant growth. Each discussion adds a layer of understanding as each season readies the plant to bloom uniquely.

Through these reflective practices, individuals learn not only about mythology but also about themselves. They identify personal growth areas and see parallels between the mythic trials of gods and heroes and their life challenges. This ongoing engagement with mythological themes cultivates a deeper emotional and spiritual wisdom, enhancing one's ability to navigate the complexities of modern life.

Reflective practices like journaling and discussion enrich our understanding of mythological themes by revealing personal parallels and fostering growth.

Finding Personal Resonance with Mythological Themes

Identifying personal experiences that resonate with themes from Egyptian mythology invites a profound connection to these ancient narratives. For instance, the story of Isis and Osiris can reflect personal themes of loss, resilience, and the quest for wholeness in one's life. Recognizing these parallels allows individuals to draw strength and inspiration from the myths, seeing them not as distant tales but as reflections of their own reality.

When you encounter a challenging situation, think of Osiris' trials. How do you piece together the scattered parts of your life, much like

Isis did for Osiris? This rhetorical question encourages introspection and personal connection to the myth.

Engaging with these stories through the lens of personal experience also allows for a transformative understanding. Each myth becomes a mirror, reflecting not just a story from the past but a living, breathing lesson highly relevant to contemporary life. This engagement is not passive but an active, dynamic process where the ancient and the modern meet.

Using an analogy, consider how a river carves its path through the landscape. Similarly, the flow of our lives is shaped by the myths we internalize, continuously carving deeper understandings and new paths of personal relevance.

This personal connection to mythology can be profoundly empowering. It provides a framework through which individuals can view their challenges and triumphs, drawing parallels with the heroic journeys of mythological figures. This not only enriches the narrative of one's life but also imbues daily experiences with a sense of purpose and historical continuity.

Could recognizing your life events in the myths of ancient Egypt reveal deeper layers of your personal journey?

Integrating Mythological Wisdom into Everyday Life

Incorporating mythological lessons into daily life is a powerful way to enhance personal fulfillment and growth. Seeing the mythical themes of courage, transformation, and renewal mirrored in daily challenges, one can approach life with renewed purpose and resilience. This integration method acts like weaving; each thread of mythological understanding is interlaced with the fabric of everyday experiences, strengthening the overall tapestry of life.

One effective method to integrate these lessons is through visualization. Imagine each day as an opportunity to embody the qualities of a mythological hero you admire. What traits would you bring into your personal and professional interactions? This practice keeps the mythological themes alive and empowers individuals to manifest these qualities in tangible ways.

Another practical approach is to use mythological stories as a basis for meditation or reflection at the end of the day. Consider what challenges you faced and how figures from mythology might have navigated similar obstacles. This provides a nightly reflection ritual and aligns personal actions with the wisdom of the ancients.

Through these daily practices, mythology becomes more than just stories; they become tools for living a more fulfilled and reflective life. Each day offers a new chapter in one's personal epic, guided by the wisdom of myth.

Integrating mythological themes into daily practices transforms ancient stories into practical personal growth and fulfillment tools.

Reflective practices are more than just a method; they are a pathway to profound personal growth and a deeper understanding of the rich tapestry of Egyptian mythology. This journey into the ancient narratives that shaped an entire civilization offers knowledge and transformative insights that can enhance our daily lives.

Step 1: Journaling is the foundation of this reflective practice. Dedicating a journal to Egyptian mythology creates a personal space to explore and connect with these ancient stories. Regular entries not only enhance your understanding but also allow you to see the reflections of these myths in your own life experiences.

Step 2: Sharing and discussion bring your insights into a communal space, enriching your perspective and deepening your connections with others who share your interests. Whether through book clubs, lectures, or online forums, these discussions can illuminate new aspects of mythology and its relevance to modern life.

Step 3: Creative expression offers a unique avenue to internalize mythological themes. Through poetry, art, or performance, you engage with these stories creatively, opening up new avenues of understanding and personal expression.

Step 4: Meditation or reflection provides a moment of introspection, allowing the lessons of the myths to resonate deeply within you. This practice can help clarify the myths' meanings and their implications for personal growth and decision-making.

Step 5: Integration into daily life is the most crucial step. It involves applying the wisdom of Egyptian mythology to everyday situations, which can lead to a more balanced, insightful, and harmonious life.

Step 6: Seek expert guidance to ensure deep expertise supports and enriches your journey. Workshops and courses can provide new insights and foster greater understanding.

Step 7: Embrace lifelong learning. This step reminds us that the journey is continuous. There is always more to learn from the rich well of Egyptian mythology, and each insight adds to our growth and understanding.

By engaging in these steps, you learn about ancient myths and weave these timeless lessons into the fabric of your daily life. This process is about looking back into history and moving forward with a richer, more enlightened perspective on life's complexities.

Chapter 7: Collective Wisdom: Building Communities through Mythological Exploration

In the warm embrace of an early morning, the small town of Alveridge greeted the day with a gentle hum. Still shy in its ascent, the sun cast a soft light over the old library where Eleanor found herself once more. She was an archivist by trade but a seeker by heart, driven by an unquenchable thirst for understanding the threads of mythology and spirituality that wove through human history.

Today was not just another day among the stacks of ancient texts and whispering pages. Today, she was preparing for the monthly meeting of the Mythos Circle, a group she had founded to explore these very themes. As she arranged chairs around a large oak table, her mind wandered to the upcoming discussion on how myths shape our understanding of community and individual purpose.

The air in the library was rich with the scent of old books—a mix of must and wisdom—that always seemed to calm her nerves while igniting her imagination. She paused, running her fingers along the spines of books that held secrets older than any living soul in Alveridge. Each tome offered stories and lifelines to those who sought meaning beyond the visible world.

Eleanor's thoughts were interrupted by footsteps—a rhythmic tap echoing through the hall as members began to arrive. James entered first, always eager, with questions that seemed to pull answers from deeper than one might expect. Maria followed, thoughtful and reflective, her insights often weaving personal experiences with philosophical musings that challenged everyone's thinking.

As they settled around the table, Eleanor initiated their discussion by sharing her recent challenge: integrating these ancient stories into modern contexts without stripping them of their essence or power. The group leaned in as she spoke, their faces mirrors of concern and curiosity.

"Think about it," she said softly yet firmly. *"How do we hold onto these narratives so that they continue to teach us about life's mysteries without becoming mere artifacts?"*

The room filled with an energizing mix: tension from confronting this dilemma and exhilaration at delving into such complex territory together. Ideas bounced back and forth, and stories were shared, from Norse gods to African spirits, each adding layers to their collective understanding.

As twilight began to paint its colors outside, Eleanor noticed how light shifted across the room. This reminded her how perspectives can change depending on where one stands—not just physically but also within one's own journey through life.

Was it possible that these myths were not only guides but also reflections of their own inner landscapes? Could engaging deeply with these tales help them navigate their paths more clearly?

Unveiling the Power of Community in Mythology

Imagine a world where each story told is heard and lived, where every myth carries an echo of ancient wisdom and a blueprint for modern community building. This is the essence of exploring mythological themes together. In Egyptian mythology, where gods and goddesses not only ruled the ancient world but also shaped its philosophy, there lies a profound opportunity to enhance our lives through collective exploration. The wisdom of the ancients isn't just historical data; it's a living, breathing guide that, when discussed and dissected within groups, illuminates personal and collective paths.

Engaging Together: More Than Just Conversation

Something remarkable happens when people gather to discuss and dissect the rich tapestries of Egyptian mythology. It's not merely an exchange of ideas but a weaving of personal experiences with communal insights. Engaging in groups or forums focused on such topics does more than broaden individual understanding—it creates a shared space where learning is multiplied. Here, every participant brings their unique perspective, adding layers to the collective knowledge and deepening the connection everyone has with these ancient narratives.

The Power of Shared Insights

Sharing personal insights and challenges within these groups offers a dual benefit. It allows for personal growth and clarity and enriches others' understanding. Each story or challenge shared adds more color and depth to the group's collective wisdom. This process highlights diverse perspectives that might remain unexplored, revealing connections between personal experiences and universal themes in mythology.

Deepening Connections Through Collective Wisdom

Community engagement in mythological studies does more than educate—it transforms. As group members delve deeper into myths, they do not simply learn about gods, rituals, or historical contexts; they learn about each other and themselves. This deepened understanding fosters stronger bonds within the group and creates a supportive network that mirrors the interconnectedness seen in the stories.

The benefits of such communal engagement are manifold. Participants often find that discussing myths in a group helps them integrate these ancient lessons more effectively into their daily lives. The myths become living wisdom, guiding principles that inform decisions and inspire actions.

Building Bridges with Ancient Stories

Through communal exploration of Egyptian mythology, individuals can find powerful reflections on modern issues—leadership, ethics, or personal transformation. The age-old struggles and triumphs of gods and mortals offer valuable lessons on resilience and adaptation that are incredibly relevant today.

Moreover, this shared journey through mythology can act as a bridge between cultures and generations. It opens up dialogues that might not otherwise occur, fostering an appreciation for historical context and contemporary relevance.

Conclusion: A Collective Journey Toward Wisdom

As we prepare to delve deeper into how community engagement enhances mythological exploration, remember that this journey is as much about building relationships as it is about building knowledge. It's about creating a space where ancient stories ignite modern transformations, fostering personal growth and communal harmony.

This chapter will explore how engaging in mythology can deepen our understanding of the past and our present community dynamics. By weaving through discussions on benefits, sharing challenges, and celebrating diverse perspectives within these groups, we embark on an enlightening path as much as it is enriching—a true testament to the power of collective wisdom.

Engaging in Mythological Communities

Participating in groups or forums focused on mythology and spirituality brings numerous benefits. These settings act as melting pots of ideas where individuals from diverse backgrounds gather to share their unique perspectives. In these gatherings, the myths of old breathe new life, transforming from ancient stories into relevant, living ideas that continue to shape our understanding of the world.

Imagine a tapestry, each thread representing a different voice or perspective within the forum. Together, these threads create a vibrant and cohesive image, much richer than any single thread could achieve. This analogy illustrates how collective engagement in mythological discussions enhances each participant's depth and breadth of understanding.

Members of these groups often report a heightened sense of connection not only to the myths themselves but also to each other. This sense of community supports individuals in their personal and spiritual growth as they explore complex philosophical ideas within a supportive network. The exchange of insights in these forums fosters a unique learning environment where questions are encouraged, and diverse viewpoints are valued.

The practical benefits are also significant. Engaging in these discussions can improve critical thinking and communication skills. As members articulate their thoughts and respond to others, they refine their ability to express complex ideas clearly and persuasively. This skill is invaluable, extending far beyond the confines of the discussion group into every area of personal and professional life.

The key benefit of engaging in mythology-focused groups is enriching understanding through shared perspectives.

Sharing Insights and Challenges

When individuals share personal insights and challenges within a group, the diversity of perspectives can lead to profound discoveries. Each member's experience adds a unique layer to the collective understanding, enabling all participants to see the myths through different cultural, philosophical, and personal lenses.

Why do these shared experiences matter? They bring about greater empathy and understanding among group members. As people open up about their challenges, others respond with support and compassion, creating a nurturing environment for personal growth.

Consider the process of sculpting a masterpiece from a block of marble. Each person's insight chisels away the superfluous, revealing the more refined truth hidden within the myth. This collaborative effort can transform a simple discussion into a powerful learning experience.

Moreover, sharing challenges often leads to collective problem-solving, where the group's creativity can overcome individual limitations. This dynamic is particularly powerful in discussions about spirituality and mythology, where interpretations are often subjective and insights deeply personal.

The practice of sharing also cultivates a deeper self-awareness among participants. As individuals articulate their thoughts and feelings, they often discover new aspects of themselves and gain clarity on their beliefs and values.

How might sharing your story within a group change your perspective or deepen your understanding?

Deepening Understanding Through Community Engagement

Community engagement in the exploration of mythology deepens individual understanding. It creates meaningful connections that transcend the typical boundaries of learning. These connections are forged in the shared journey through ancient wisdom, where every discussion and debate can lead to a deeper communal bond.

Like gardeners tending to a shared plot, each member contributes knowledge and effort, collectively leading to a flourishing understanding. This analogy highlights the collaborative nature of learning in community settings, where the collective effort yields a richer harvest of knowledge and insight.

Engaging with others in these discussions often leads to surprising revelations, as different interpretations and viewpoints challenge and expand one's thinking. This dynamic environment encourages participants to explore ideas they might not have considered on their own, fostering personal and intellectual growth.

The connections made in these communities often extend beyond the discussions themselves, providing a network of support and encouragement. This network can be precious when exploring complex and usually challenging spiritual and philosophical terrain.

By engaging in mythological communities, individuals deepen their understanding and contribute to collective wisdom, creating meaningful connections that enrich everyone involved.

Engaging in communities centered around mythology and spirituality is not merely an academic pursuit but a journey into the shared human experience. Participating in groups or forums reaps the benefits of collective wisdom, dramatically enhancing our comprehension and appreciation of ancient teachings. This shared journey fosters personal growth and creates a tapestry of perspectives that enrich each member's understanding.

Community engagement is fundamental in breathing life into the age-old stories and philosophies that might otherwise seem distant or disconnected from our modern existence. When we ***share our personal insights*** and face challenges together, we unlock a more profound connection to these narratives, seeing them not just as tales of the past but as living, evolving dialogues that still resonate with our contemporary lives.

The process of group exploration allows us to ***gain diverse perspectives,*** which is invaluable. Each individual brings a unique lens shaped by their experiences, and this diversity enriches the dialogue, allowing for a more comprehensive exploration than one could achieve alone. Through this kaleidoscope of views, myths regain their power, influencing us in deeply personal and collective ways.

Moreover, these interactions foster ***meaningful connections*** beyond the intellectual, touching the spiritual and emotional realms. The bonds formed through shared curiosity and mutual respect for ancient wisdom create a supportive community. This network nurtures our intellectual curiosity and provides emotional support as we navigate the complexities of integrating these ancient lessons into our daily lives.

As we move forward, let us remember that mythology is not static; it is dynamic and responsive to the communal energies that engage with it. By participating in these groups, we do more than learn—we participate in the living history of human thought. We breathe new life into stories told for millennia, reinvigorating them with our contemporary insights and challenges.

Let this be a call to action: embrace the opportunity to explore mythology within a community setting. The wisdom of the ancients is not locked in old texts but waits to be unlocked through dialogue and shared exploration. In doing so, we not only discover more about these myths but also more about ourselves and each other, continuing the ever-evolving journey of human understanding and connection.

Chapter 8: Myth in Motion: Creatively Engaging with Egyptian Myths

In the dimly lit studio, cluttered with canvases and the scent of drying oil paint, Sarah stood back from her latest creation—a vast canvas depicting the ancient Egyptian goddess Isis spreading her wings in protection. Each stroke of her brush had been a whisper into the past, an attempt to connect with a myth that seemed impossibly distant and intensely personal.

Her fascination with Egyptian mythology began as a child but deepened when she lost her mother. The myths about Isis and her relentless quest to resurrect Osiris became a tapestry onto which she cast her grief and hope. Art was her way of weaving her own story into those ancient narratives.

Outside, the city thrummed with life; horns blared, and people shouted to one another across busy streets. But inside Sarah's studio, time moved differently. Here, it was as if the modern world could wait, pressing pause while she explored an era when gods walked among men.

As she mixed a shade of blue reminiscent of lapis lazuli used in royal Egyptian jewelry, Sarah thought about how Isis's story resonated with her own—both were tales of loss and resurrection. It wasn't just about learning or teaching mythology; it was about living through it, letting the old stories lend strength to her own.

A friend once asked why she immersed herself so deeply in ancient lore when the world around her offered newer stories to tell. She replied simply that these myths helped anchor her to history, humanity, and herself.

The day waned into the evening as Sarah added final touches to Isis's feathers. The room grew darker; only the soft glow from a single lamp illuminated her work now. She stepped back again, considering the finished piece before her and what it represented: an interplay between learning and personal growth through creative expression.

What other ancient stories might we draw personal strength from if we allowed ourselves this same creative exploration?

Unleashing Your Inner Creator Through Ancient Myths

When one delves into the rich tapestry of Egyptian mythology, they uncover not just stories of gods and mortals but also timeless wisdom that has pervaded centuries. *Engaging creatively* with these myths opens up a personal avenue to appreciate and internalize these ancient narratives. This chapter will explore how personal creative expression—through writing, drawing, or performance—can transform your understanding and appreciation of these stories.

With its complex characters and intricate plots, Egyptian mythology provides a fertile ground for creative exploration. Individuals can explore various facets of their personality and gain deeper insights into their lives by *writing poems*, crafting stories, or creating visual art inspired by these myths. This form of engagement is not merely about recreation; it's an enriching process that connects us more deeply to the past while allowing us to reflect on our present.

Through personal experience and anecdotal evidence, we'll discuss how such creative endeavors are not just acts of expression but also profound learning experiences. When you translate a myth into a painting or script, you're not just retelling a story but embodying the ethos and lessons embedded within it. This act of creation makes the myth relevant to contemporary life, bridging the gap between ancient wisdom and modern existence.

Moreover, this chapter will highlight how these creative processes do more than entertain; they personalize the learning experience. When you sketch Thoth, the god of wisdom and writing, you engage with the concept of knowledge itself. When you write from the perspective of

Isis, you explore themes of loyalty, power, and resurrection. This personal connection ensures that the mythological teachings are **understood and *felt*** on a visceral level.

We'll also analyze how sharing these creative outputs can further enrich one's engagement with mythology. Whether through community art projects, school performances, or social media posts, sharing your creations invites dialogue and reflection from others and within yourself. It fosters a communal learning environment where myths are heard and experienced collectively.

In essence, this chapter will serve as both a guide and an inspiration for those looking to deepen their connection with Egyptian mythology through creativity. The aim is to show that individuals can foster a deeper understanding of themselves and the world around them by engaging actively with these myths.

By embracing this creative journey, you are not only keeping these ancient stories alive but also allowing them to evolve within your own life narrative. Thus, through creativity, old wisdom finds new expressions and continues to enlighten us in ways that are as surprising as they are profound.

Exploring Different Forms of Creative Expression

With its rich tapestry of gods, goddesses, and mythical narratives, Egyptian mythology offers a fertile ground for creative expression. Writing, drawing, and performing are just a few mediums to explore these ancient stories. Engaging with mythology through writing allows one to weave personal interpretations into the traditional myths, creating a unique narrative that resonates on an individual level.

Like a painter blending colors on a canvas, drawing myths imbues them with new hues of understanding. Illustrating scenes from Egyptian mythology brings the stories to life. It allows the artist to embed personal symbolism and style into the depiction. This process doesn't just recreate the myths; it revitalizes them.

Performing myths through dance, theatre, or oral storytelling transforms the static words of ancient texts into dynamic, living expressions. Each performance is a reinterpretation, a new lens through which audiences can engage with these age-old tales. This preserves the mythology and makes it accessible and relatable to contemporary audiences.

Through these creative outlets, Egyptian myths are not just passed down but reimagined and reinvigorated. This active engagement helps preserve these stories for future generations while making them deeply personal for the creator.

Creative expression allows for a personal connection with Egyptian mythology, making ancient stories more relevant and alive today.

Personalizing Mythology Through Creative Pursuits

Creative pursuits offer a unique pathway to personalizing the learning and appreciation of Egyptian mythology. By engaging in activities such as writing, drawing, or performing, individuals imbue these ancient stories with their own emotions, thoughts, and perspectives. This personal touch transforms the myths from distant tales into relevant, living stories.

Consider the impact of writing your own version of an ancient myth. This act demands an understanding of the original narrative and invites you to consider what the myth means to you. How does the story reflect your own experiences, fears, or aspirations? In this way, the myth becomes a mirror, reflecting your life back at you through the guise of gods and monsters.

Drawing, too, allows for a deep, personal connection with the myths. As you sketch the feathered wings of Isis or the stern visage of Osiris, you are not just replicating an image; you are interpreting and reshaping the myth through your artistic lens. Each stroke adds a layer of personal interpretation, coloring the ancient stories with your emotional and aesthetic sensibilities.

Performing a myth can be an equally transformative experience. By embodying the characters of Egyptian mythology, you bring them to life in a way that is uniquely yours. Each gesture and intonation adds depth to the narrative, making the ancient deities and their tales resonate with a modern audience.

Through these creative endeavors, the myths of Egypt become not just stories from the past but a vibrant part of the present. They evolve and grow with each new interpretation, enriched by the personal insights and creativity of those who engage with them.

By personalizing these ancient narratives, we discover hidden parts of ourselves.

Deepening Consciousness Through Creative Outputs

Creating based on Egyptian mythology does more than entertain; it deepens our consciousness and embeds these ancient teachings into our modern lives. When we engage creatively with mythology, we do not just learn about the gods and their stories; we experience them. This experiential learning fosters a deeper understanding and appreciation of the myths.

Writing a story based on a myth, for instance, requires diving deep into the symbolism and themes of the ancient narratives. This exploration is akin to walking through a once-forgotten garden, discovering its hidden paths and secret corners. Through writing, these hidden elements of the myth become apparent, and their wisdom is more profoundly understood.

Drawing or painting scenes from mythology also deepens our connection to these stories. As we visualize and give form to the abstract, the myths take on a new life. This process is not just about creating art;

it's about embedding the essence of the myths into our visual and spatial memory.

Performing myths through dance, theater, or spoken word allows us to embody the deities and their stories. This physical embodiment brings the myths into our bodily experience, creating a powerful connection that transcends intellectual understanding.

These creative expressions do more than recount tales from long ago; they make these stories part of who we are today. By engaging with Egyptian mythology creatively, we allow these ancient teachings to influence our modern lives, guiding us with their timeless wisdom.

Through writing, drawing, and performing, we preserve Egyptian mythology, allowing it to evolve and enrich our contemporary consciousness.

Creative expression is a powerful conduit for deeply engaging Egyptian mythology. By choosing to explore these ancient stories through various forms of art, we not only enrich our understanding but also personalize them, making them resonate more profoundly in our modern lives. This chapter has highlighted the transformative potential of intertwining creativity with mythological exploration, suggesting that when we bring these stories into our creative processes, they gain new life and relevance.

Engaging Creatively with Myths: A Step-by-Step Guide

The journey of creative expression begins with selecting a form that aligns with your interests, whether writing, drawing, performing, or another medium. This choice is crucial as it sets the foundation for how you interact with the myths. Next, choosing a specific myth or theme that sparks your curiosity or passion is essential. This connection ensures your creative endeavors are infused with genuine interest and personal significance.

Research is a pivotal step, as a deep understanding of your chosen myth provides the necessary context and enriches your creative output. This background knowledge allows for a more authentic and informed artistic expression. Brainstorming then opens the door to innovation, enabling you to visualize or verbalize unique perspectives that may not have been explored.

The actual creation process is where your ideas and concepts materialize, bringing the ancient myths into a contemporary form.

This step is where your personal voice and interpretation play critical roles in reshaping the narrative. Reflection upon completion of your work ensures that it truly reflects the essence of the myth and your understanding of it.

Sharing and engaging with others about your work validates your efforts and enhances your understanding through diverse perspectives. Exhibiting or performing your work publicly can amplify the impact of the myth, reaching more people and inspiring them to embark on their own creative explorations.

Finally, documenting and preserving this journey is a testament to your personal growth and creative exploration. It holds the potential to inspire future projects and reflect your journey through the realms of Egyptian mythology.

Through this structured yet flexible process, you're not just creating art but also embedding ancient wisdom into contemporary life, ensuring that these age-old stories continue to inspire and educate.

This approach does not merely preserve history; it revives and evolves it, allowing us to connect with our past in the most personal and innovative ways.

By embracing this creative pathway, we forge a deeper connection with the past that is both enlightening and transformative, proving that Egyptian myths still hold relevant lessons and boundless inspiration for our modern world.

Chapter 9: Universal Truths: The Wider Implications of Egyptian Mythological Studies

In the dim warmth of an early Egyptian morning, Amun paced along the bank of the Nile, his mind as turbulent as the river's currents. Today, unlike any other day, he carried with him not just his fishing nets but a heavy heart burdened with existential musings. His father had passed into the realm of Anubis just a fortnight ago, leaving words that stirred like a storm in Amun's soul: *"Seek wisdom in the myths of our ancestors; therein lies the essence of life."*

The sun climbed higher, casting golden hues over the papyrus reeds that swayed gently by the riverside. Amun's thoughts drifted to Osiris, the god of death and resurrection. He pondered on how Osiris' dismemberment by his brother Set and subsequent reassembly by Isis mirrored his own shattered reality and quest for wholeness after his father's demise. Was life merely a cycle of breaking and mending?

A soft wind carried whispers across the water, ripples touching Amun's bare feet like cold fingers from the underworld. It reminded him of Isis' undying love and magic that breathed life into Osiris. Perhaps there was a lesson in this myth—about enduring love and rebirth through loss.

He cast his net more forcefully than necessary, watching it fan out and disappear into the murky depths. As he waited for a catch, he thought about Ma'at—the goddess of truth and order—and her role in maintaining balance in celestial and mundane realms. His world felt imbalanced; could these ancient beliefs help recalibrate his life's compass?

A fish struggled within the confines of Amun's net—a silvery flash against dark waters. He pulled it up gently, contemplating how every creature played its part in this vast tapestry of existence, each bound to their fate yet contributing to universal harmony.

As he unhooked the fish under Anubis' watchful eye painted on his boat bow, Amun wondered if understanding these myths could fortify one against life's unpredictable currents. Could these stories from ages past offer solace or even guidance for living meaningfully amidst the chaos?

Amidst nature's simple yet profound theater—where land met water under an ever-watchful sky—could one really find answers written in age-old myths? Or were they mere reflections of our perennial search for meaning?

Unveiling Timeless Wisdom: How Ancient Egyptian Myths Shape Our Modern Lives

Ancient Egyptian mythology, often shrouded in mystery and grandeur, extends far beyond the tales of gods and pharaohs. It holds the key to understanding deeper philosophical and existential questions that resonate with us today. This chapter delves into how these age-old stories enrich our knowledge of a past civilization and illuminate universal truths about the human condition. By exploring these myths, we can uncover insights that promote a more reflective and meaningful personal life.

The myths of ancient Egypt serve as more than just historical or religious artifacts; they are mirrors reflecting the perennial concerns of humanity. From tales of creation to the complex narratives of death and rebirth, these stories tackle life's biggest questions: Who are we? Why are we here? What happens after we die? These narratives offer a unique opportunity to engage with ideas contemplated by humans across millennia.

In this exploration, we will discuss how these myths articulate universal truths about existence, morality, and human nature through their gods and symbols. For instance, the story of Isis and Osiris touches on themes of love, betrayal, and redemption—themes that are still very much relevant in today's world. By understanding how the ancients interpreted these experiences, we can gain new perspectives on our own lives.

Moreover, engaging with these ancient stories encourages us to reflect on our personal journeys. In a world that often values speed over depth, taking the time to ponder these age-old lessons can be particularly grounding. It invites us to slow down and consider what is truly important.

We will also identify practical ways in which the wisdom embedded in Egyptian mythology can be integrated into contemporary life. Whether the concept of Ma'at (*balance and order*) influences our pursuit of personal and social harmony or Anubis' role in the afterlife shapes our understanding of mortality and legacy, there is much to learn from how the Egyptians viewed their world.

This chapter aims to educate and inspire. Through a thoughtful examination of Egyptian mythology, you are invited to discover pathways toward personal growth and greater self-awareness. Let us embark on this journey together, uncovering the timeless lessons hidden within these ancient myths.

As we navigate these themes, remember that the goal is not merely academic but profoundly personal. By reconnecting with these universal truths, you are stepping into a stream of wisdom that has flowed through human consciousness for thousands of years. This genuinely transformative experience beckons you to look inward and outward in your quest for understanding.

Exploring the Broader Philosophical and Existential Questions Addressed by Egyptian Mythology

Egyptian mythology, with its rich tapestry of gods, goddesses, and mythical narratives, is more than just ancient lore. At its core, these stories address profound philosophical and existential questions that resonate deeply with what it means to be human. Themes of creation, morality, and the afterlife are not just ancient concerns but universal, timeless issues that continue to challenge and inspire.

Imagine a world where every action and decision is influenced by the divine. In ancient Egypt, mythology was not a distant and dusty relic. Still, it was woven into the everyday lives of its people. This integration transformed their understanding of the world around them, offering explanations for natural events and guiding their philosophical outlook on life and death.

The myths often explored questions of existence, such as why we are here and what happens after we die. For instance, the myth of Osiris, who was killed and then resurrected, brings up existential questions about death and rebirth, literally and metaphorically. It encourages individuals to reflect on their lives and the cycles of nature and existence.

Ancient Egyptians contemplated the cosmos and their place within it through these stories, shaping their cultural and societal values. Such reflection is not just an academic exercise but a profound personal exploration that can lead to greater self-awareness and understanding.

The enduring power of these myths lies in their ability to connect on a human level across centuries and cultures. They provide a mirror to our lives, reflecting back at us our fears and hopes and our infinite potential to rethink and reshape our understanding of the world.

Egyptian mythology opens the door to enduring existential and philosophical questions, inviting us to explore profound truths about our existence.

Discussing How Ancient Myths Illuminate Universal Truths About the Human Condition

The stories the ancient Egyptians tell are far from mere entertainment; they are imbued with insights into the human condition. Consider the myth of Isis and Osiris: a tale of love, betrayal, and redemption that speaks to the core experiences of loss, resilience, and the quest for justice. This story, among others, contains layers of meaning that still talk to us today about the complexities of human emotions and relationships.

Myths serve as timeless reflections on human nature, revealing universal truths about our strengths and vulnerabilities. They articulate the complexities of emotions and social bonds, helping us understand and navigate our relationships and societal roles.

How do these ancient stories, set in a world so different from our own, resonate with us on such a deep level? They grapple with the fundamental aspects of human experience—love, power, betrayal, and recovery. These are not merely Egyptian themes; they are human themes.

Using an analogy, consider the myth of the sun god Ra, who travels through the underworld each night to be reborn at dawn. This can be seen as a metaphor for human resilience—the idea that each day allows us to renew ourselves, to rise again from our own challenges and darkness.

By examining these myths, we learn not only about the ancients but also about ourselves. They hold up a mirror to our modern lives, highlighting our aspirations, fears, and greatest potential.

In these ancient narratives, we find the reflections of our own modern souls.

Identifying How These Teachings Can Lead to a More Reflective and Meaningful Personal Life

The wisdom embedded in Egyptian mythology can significantly influence our personal growth and reflection. Engaging with these ancient stories allows us to develop a deeper appreciation for life's complexities and a more nuanced understanding of our own experiences.

Take, for example, the concept of Ma'at, or balance and harmony, which was central to Egyptian belief systems. This principle encourages fairness and truth and can guide us in creating a more balanced life, emphasizing integrity and harmony in our personal and professional relationships.

Imagine integrating the principle of Ma'at into daily life. It's like maintaining balance in a boat on a vast river. Just as the Egyptians revered the Nile for its life-giving resources, we can view our actions and choices as contributing to the flow of our lives, keeping us steady and directed toward our goals.

By reflecting on these principles, we can cultivate a mindset that values balance and harmony, leading to a more thoughtful and intentional approach to life. This can ultimately enhance our relationships, work, and understanding of ourselves.

Incorporating these ancient teachings into modern life doesn't require us to build temples or perform rituals; instead, it invites us to build temples of understanding and perform rituals of reflection.

Exploring Egyptian mythology, discussing its universal truths, and applying its wisdom can enhance our understanding of the human condition and lead more reflective, meaningful lives.

With its rich narratives and symbolic complexity, Egyptian mythology serves as a profound gateway to understanding deeper truths about existence and the human spirit. Through exploring these ancient stories, we've seen how they address broad philosophical and existential questions that remain relevant today.

These myths offer insights into life, death, love, and justice, reminding us that the fundamental aspects of human experience are universal and timeless.

Reflecting on these myths encourages us to see beyond the superficial aspects of daily life and to embrace a more reflective approach to our existence. By understanding the trials and triumphs of figures like Osiris and Isis, we gain a deeper appreciation for the cycles of life and the resilience required to navigate them. These stories teach us about the past and illuminate the common threads that connect all human beings.

The teachings embedded in Egyptian mythology have practical implications for personal growth and fulfillment. We can cultivate qualities like courage, wisdom, and compassion by applying these age-old truths to our modern lives. ***This process of reflection is not just about learning from the past; it's about actively shaping a more meaningful future.***

As we move forward, let us carry the lessons learned from these ancient narratives. Let them inspire us to lead richer and more reflective lives filled with a deeper understanding of the universal human journey. Embracing this wisdom can transform our personal experiences and lead us to live with greater purpose and insight.

This exploration of Egyptian mythology is not merely academic but a journey towards self-discovery and enlightenment. Integrating these timeless truths into our daily lives enhances our capacity for introspection and understanding of the world around us. Let us continue to draw inspiration from these ancient tales and allow them to guide us in our quest for knowledge and personal evolution.

Chapter 10: Leading with Legends: How Ancient Myths Shape Modern Leaders

In the dim light of the early morning, Thomas stood alone in the vast hall of the museum, surrounded by towering statues and ancient relics from a time when gods walked among men, at least in the minds of those who carved their likenesses into stone. Today was no ordinary day for Thomas; he was preparing for an exhibition that would unveil Egyptian mythology to a modern audience hungry for wisdom and guidance from the past.

He walked slowly between the exhibits, his fingers brushing against the cool stone of a scribe's statue. He thought about Thoth, the god of wisdom, who inventoried the universe and gave humans the gift of writing. *"Could leaders today learn from Thoth's discipline and insight?"* he wondered silently, pondering how such ancient mythologies could be applied to contemporary leadership challenges—transparency, ethics, and decision-making under pressure.

As Thomas adjusted the lighting over a papyrus displaying hieroglyphics of Ma'at—the goddess representing truth and balance—he considered how her principles could influence societal development today. Ma'at's feather symbolizing truth could provide a symbolic balance scale in an era filled with conflicts and disparities. *"What if our leaders were judged against the weight of truth as Ma'at did with human hearts?"* he mused.

His reverie was broken by footsteps echoing through the hall. Clara, his colleague, approached with notes for the upcoming panel discussion. They spoke briefly about logistics but soon reflected on how a disciplined study of these myths might offer personal wisdom. Clara shared her fascination with Isis, admired for her determination and magical prowess in reassembling Osiris.

"Imagine harnessing that resolve in facing our own life's fragmentations," she said thoughtfully.

The conversation shifted as they walked towards Sekhmet's statue—a lioness goddess embodying strength and healing through ferocity. Thomas noted how fear often held back potential growth within communities. *"Could we channel Sekhmet's fierce energy into courageous actions for communal welfare?"* he proposed as they examined her imposing figure.

Leaving Clara to finalize some details, Thomas stepped outside where dawn had broken fully, casting golden hues over Cairo's skyline visible from their museum on its elevated perch. The city thrummed below—a modern metropolis continuously molded by its rich past yet facing modern-day challenges like any other global city.

As he watched the sun ascend further into the sky, Thomas contemplated how systematically engaging with Egyptian mythology might not only enrich individual lives but also guide entire communities towards sustainable development rooted in ancient wisdom yet relevant to today's global issues.

Could we find our way forward by looking back?

Unveiling Timeless Leadership: How Ancient Myths Craft Tomorrow's Visionaries

The profound narratives of Egyptian mythology, often relegated to academic study or museum exhibits, hold invaluable lessons for contemporary leadership and societal development. As we delve into these ancient tales, we uncover the rich tapestry of Egyptian culture and practical wisdom that is remarkably applicable to modern challenges. This exploration is not merely an academic exercise but a journey toward harnessing a legacy of knowledge that can profoundly influence today's world.

Ancient Archetypes for Modern Mastery

Egyptian mythology presents a pantheon of deities whose characteristics and stories are not just fascinating relics but are exemplars of leadership qualities that are highly relevant today.

Figures such as Osiris, the god of resurrection and regenerative power, and Isis, the goddess of wisdom and motherhood, embody traits such as resilience, strategic thinking, and nurturing leadership. These mythological figures offer more than just stories; they provide ***models for behavior and decision-making*** that can guide current and future leaders in various fields.

Disciplined Wisdom: Beyond Mere Knowledge

The systematic study of these myths does more than expand our historical knowledge. It enriches our personal wisdom and provides nuanced insights into human nature and governance. This disciplined approach to understanding Egyptian myths can transform personal development by offering enduring lessons on virtue, justice, and power dynamics. It is about cultivating a mindset that appreciates depth and complexity, encouraging leaders to think profoundly about their actions and impacts.

Societal Harmony Through Mythological Insights

Moreover, the implications of these ancient stories extend beyond individual growth to influence wider communal and societal development. Understanding the moral and ethical frameworks within which these myths operate allows communities to foster a greater sense of unity and purpose. The principles derived from ancient Egyptian wisdom can help craft policies promoting social harmony and collective wellbeing.

Reflecting on the overarching themes of our exploration into Egyptian wisdom, we see a consistent thread: the ability of ancient insights to inform and improve modern life. From personal growth to enhancing community bonds, the strategic application of lessons from

Egyptian mythology offers a holistic blueprint for advancement in contemporary society.

The Echoes That Shape Us

As we progress through this exploration, it becomes evident that these stories are not trapped in the sands of time but are vibrant echoes that continue to resonate with us today. They encourage us to look back and move forward more wisely. Engaging with these legends teaches us about resilience in the face of chaos, integrity in leadership, and the importance of balance between various aspects of life.

This chapter will explore how these timeless narratives can be specifically applied to cultivate leadership qualities, enhance personal wisdom, and contribute positively to societal development. Through reflective examination and thoughtful application, we aim to draw practical insights from a civilization that has mastered the art over millennia.

By integrating these age-old lessons into modern contexts, we pay homage to our cultural heritage and build foundations for future generations to thrive. Thus, engaging with Egyptian mythology is more than a scholarly pursuit—it is a transformative journey that beckons us to lead with legends.

Exploring Egyptian Mythological Figures as Models for Contemporary Leadership

Egyptian mythology is a treasure trove of characters whose traits and stories offer invaluable lessons for modern leaders. Figures such as Osiris, the god of regeneration and rebirth, exemplify resilience and vision, essential to effective leadership. Osiris's story of overcoming betrayal and death to become the ruler of the afterlife inspires leaders to face challenges head-on and emerge stronger.

In the business world, a leader like Osiris would be akin to a CEO steering a company through a significant crisis, transforming challenges into stepping stones for revival and future prosperity.

This analogy highlights how ancient myths can serve as a blueprint for navigating the complex landscape of contemporary leadership.

Isis, Osiris's consort, is revered for her intelligence, cunning, and problem-solving skills, which she used to reassemble Osiris's body and bring him back to life. Today's leaders can emulate her strategic thinking and resourcefulness to foster innovation and manage resources effectively.

Leadership, like the weaving of Isis's spell, involves assembling the scattered pieces of a project or team and revitalizing them to function as a cohesive whole. It's about seeing beyond the immediate to the potential in reconfiguration and renewal.

Thoth, the god of wisdom and writing, symbolizes the importance of knowledge and communication in leadership. His ability to arbitrate among gods demonstrates the power of effective communication and diplomacy in resolving conflicts and leading diverse teams.

Egyptian deities exemplify resilience, strategic thinking, and effective communication, making them outstanding models for contemporary leadership.

The Impact of Disciplined Study of Egyptian Myths on Personal Wisdom and Guidance

Disciplining Egyptian myths can significantly deepen personal wisdom and enhance leadership capabilities. By engaging with these stories, individuals gain insights into human nature, ethics, and the dynamics of power and responsibility. This systematic approach to learning from mythology cultivates a reflective and insightful mindset, essential for personal and professional growth.

Why do these ancient narratives resonate so strongly with modern audiences? They reflect universal truths about human aspirations, fears, and values. The story of Horus, for example, is not just about his battle with Set but about the eternal struggle between order and chaos, a theme that is ever-relevant.

Horus's perseverance and commitment to justice in the face of adversity are particularly instructive. Leaders can draw on his example to maintain their integrity and purpose, even when the going gets tough.

This commitment can be seen as holding the helm of a ship in stormy seas—steady and unyielded despite the tumult around. Such stories provide not only strategies but also moral courage.

By analyzing these myths, individuals can develop a nuanced understanding of leadership qualities such as Horus's vision or Isis's strategic acumen. This knowledge forms a framework within which they can evaluate and enhance their leadership approach.

Could delving deeper into these mythological worlds be the key to unlocking your leadership potential?

Implications of Mythological Wisdom on Societal and Communal Development

The ALIGN Model

The *ALIGN model* provides a structured approach to integrating the wisdom of Egyptian mythology into leadership practices. This model includes four phases: Analysis, Adaptation, Application, and Evaluation, each crucial for transforming ancient insights into modern success.

Analysis Phase

In this initial phase, leaders identify a specific challenge and then select an Egyptian deity whose story resonates with the nature of this issue. For instance, a merger leader might look to Isis for inspiration on integration and rejuvenation. Leaders extract relevant traits and strategies by analyzing the deity's actions and decisions.

Adaptation Phase

Here, the traits identified are adapted to fit contemporary contexts. This might involve using Ma'at's principle of balance to navigate the complexities of fair decision-making in business. Leaders brainstorm and creatively consider how these age-old virtues can address modern-day challenges.

Application Phase

The adapted traits are incorporated into daily leadership practices during the application phase. This could involve setting new policies that reflect the justice of Ma'at or adopting Thoth's diplomatic communication style. Leaders develop strategies to embody these traits, enhancing their effectiveness and influence.

Evaluation Phase

Finally, the evaluation phase involves assessing the impact of these myth-inspired strategies on personal leadership development, team dynamics, and overall organizational outcomes. Leaders might hold regular reflection sessions or seek feedback to gauge progress and make necessary adjustments.

The *ALIGN model* facilitates a deeper connection to ancient wisdom and fosters a dynamic and reflective leadership style that can evolve and respond to an ever-changing world.

The disciplined pursuit of Egyptian mythology, systematic personal growth, and societal enhancement are interconnected.

By embodying the virtues of mythological figures, leaders can forge paths that honor ancient wisdom and modern necessities.

Through this book's journey, we have delved deeply into the rich tapestry of Egyptian mythology, uncovering the timeless wisdom embedded in its legends and stories. The final chapter has demonstrated how these ancient narratives can serve as powerful models for contemporary leadership, enhancing personal wisdom and contributing significantly to societal and communal development.

The disciplined study of Egyptian mythology offers more than just historical insights; it provides practical guidance for modern-day challenges. By exploring the characteristics of mythological figures, leaders today can adopt traits of resilience, wisdom, and justice, much needed in our complex world. This exploration is not merely academic but a transformative experience that enriches one's personal and professional life.

Moreover, engaging with these myths systematically is akin to uncovering a map of hidden treasures. It's a journey that demands patience and curiosity but rewards with profound insights and guidance. This disciplined pursuit not only serves the individual but also has the potential to foster a community that values deep wisdom and shared learning.

The implications of mythological wisdom on societal development are vast. As we have seen, these stories offer frameworks for understanding human behavior, ethics, and values that transcend time. They encourage a society that upholds virtues that promote harmony and progress. In embracing these ancient lessons, communities can build foundations that are both culturally rich and morally robust.

This book has aimed to bridge the gap between the ancient and the modern, showing that Egyptian mythology is not a forgotten chapter of history but a living source of inspiration. By integrating the lessons from the past into our daily lives, we open ourselves to a reservoir of wisdom that can inspire change, guide leadership, and enrich our communal interactions.

Let us carry forward the knowledge that Egyptian myths are not merely stories from the past but are echoes of timeless wisdom resonating through the ages. They remind us that the human quest for meaning and excellence remains unchanged in every era. By re-engaging with these ancient narratives, we reaffirm our commitment to a life of deeper understanding, purposeful leadership, and collective wellbeing.

Embrace these lessons as both a shield and a beacon as you navigate the complexities of modern life. Let the wisdom of the ancients illuminate your path today and inspire generations to come.

Epilogue

A Journey Through Time: Reclaiming Ancient Wisdom

As we draw the curtains on our exploration of Egyptian wisdom, let us pause and reflect on our profound journey together. Through the sands of time, the myths and legends of ancient Egypt have whispered to us not as echoes of a distant past but as vibrant, living wisdom that can guide us in our modern lives.

The real-world applications of these ancient teachings are manifold and deeply relevant. Whether navigating personal challenges, seeking deeper spiritual connections, or striving for professional growth, the principles distilled from the myths of Isis, Osiris, and their divine kin offer powerful insights. These stories teach us resilience, balance, justice, and the eternal quest for knowledge.

We've delved into how these myths can illuminate our understanding of life's cycles — birth, death, and rebirth — and how they can help us foster a sense of continuity with our ancestors and the universe. This perspective encourages us to live harmoniously and purposefully within our communities and natural environments.

To truly integrate these lessons into your life, ***reflect*** on the stories that resonated most deeply with you. Consider keeping a journal where you can explore how these myths mirror your own life experiences and challenges. Engage with others who share your interest in mythology or spirituality; community discussions can significantly enhance your insights and applications.

However, I must acknowledge that my interpretations of Egyptian mythology have limitations. Further research and dialogue with archaeology, history, and theology scholars might shed even more light on these ancient narratives. I encourage you to continue exploring with an open mind and heart.

Let this book be a catalyst for your personal transformation. Embrace change as Osiris did in his resurrection — boldly and with open arms. As you turn each new page in your life, carry forward the wisdom of the ancients. Let their understanding deepen yours.

Remember that every step forward is a step into history's vast continuum. We learn from the past not because we ought to live in it but because it has much to teach us about living now — more thoughtfully, joyfully, and completely.

"The only true wisdom is in knowing you know nothing."

— Socrates

This quote from Socrates encapsulates our journey: a continuous quest for knowledge where understanding deepens through acknowledging our limitations. As you close this book, may you open your heart to endless learning and unbounded possibilities inspired by the ancients.

Don't miss out!

Visit the website below and you can sign up to receive emails whenever Myrddin Sage publishes a new book. There's no charge and no obligation.

https://books2read.com/r/B-A-JBAOB-VHEWE

BOOKS 2 READ

Connecting independent readers to independent writers.

Also by Myrddin Sage

Echoes of the Ancient: Unlocking the Mysteries of Celtic Myth
Mythic Japan: Unlocking the Legends of Gods and Heroes
Echoes of Enchantment: Navigating the Magic of Celtic Mythology
Warriors and Wizards: The Heroes of Celtic Myth
Echoes of Valhalla: Unveiling the Modern Wisdom of Norse Myths
Gods Among Us: The Power and Intrigue of Roman Mythology
The Sword and the Sage: Unveiling the Truth of Excalibur and Merlin
Myth Unleashed: Rediscovering the Legends of Hercules and the
Pantheon
Echoes of the Gods: Rediscovering the Heroes and Deities of Ancient
Egypt
Ancient Echoes: Embracing Egyptian Wisdom in Our Modern World

About the Author

At 67, Myrddin Sage steps into the spotlight as a newly published author, bringing a tapestry of rich life experiences and a vibrant imagination. His journey from a Navy Veteran to a Retired Dispatcher of Messengers has endowed him with profound insights into human cultures and the natural world. As Myrddin introduces his debut novel, he shares a narrative infused with wisdom, whimsy, and a deep respect for the interconnectedness of life. Drawing on his academic background and extensive travels, Myrddin's work explores themes of adventure, discovery, and the transformative power of knowledge. With his first publication, he proves that new chapters can be embarked upon at any stage of life, inspiring readers with the message that it is always the right time to follow one's passions.

www.ingramcontent.com/pod-product-compliance
Lightning Source LLC
Chambersburg PA
CBHW022051150726
47990CB00003B/1046

Also by Myrddin Sage

Echoes of the Ancient: Unlocking the Mysteries of Celtic Myth
Mythic Japan: Unlocking the Legends of Gods and Heroes
Echoes of Enchantment: Navigating the Magic of Celtic Mythology
Warriors and Wizards: The Heroes of Celtic Myth
Echoes of Valhalla: Unveiling the Modern Wisdom of Norse Myths
Gods Among Us: The Power and Intrigue of Roman Mythology
The Sword and the Sage: Unveiling the Truth of Excalibur and Merlin
Myth Unleashed: Rediscovering the Legends of Hercules and the Pantheon
Echoes of the Gods: Rediscovering the Heroes and Deities of Ancient Egypt
Ancient Echoes: Embracing Egyptian Wisdom in Our Modern World

About the Author

At 67, Myrddin Sage steps into the spotlight as a newly published author, bringing a tapestry of rich life experiences and a vibrant imagination. His journey from a Navy Veteran to a Retired Dispatcher of Messengers has endowed him with profound insights into human cultures and the natural world. As Myrddin introduces his debut novel, he shares a narrative infused with wisdom, whimsy, and a deep respect for the interconnectedness of life. Drawing on his academic background and extensive travels, Myrddin's work explores themes of adventure, discovery, and the transformative power of knowledge. With his first publication, he proves that new chapters can be embarked upon at any stage of life, inspiring readers with the message that it is always the right time to follow one's passions.

9 798227 730015